INTERNET THEORY, TECHNOLOGY AND APPLICATIONS

INTERNET GOVERNANCE

U.S. ROLE AND PROPOSED TRANSITION ISSUES

INTERNET THEORY, TECHNOLOGY AND APPLICATIONS

Additional books in this series can be found on Nova's website under the Series tab.

Additional e-books in this series can be found on Nova's website under the eBooks tab.

INTERNET THEORY, TECHNOLOGY AND APPLICATIONS

INTERNET GOVERNANCE

U.S. ROLE AND PROPOSED TRANSITION ISSUES

ERNESTINE SAUNDERS
EDITOR

nova
publishers
New York

Library of Congress Cataloging-in-Publication Data

ISBN: 978-1-63484-920-3

Published by Nova Science Publishers, Inc. † New York

CONTENTS

PREFACE

The Internet is often described as a "network of networks" because it is not a single physical entity, but hundreds of thousands of interconnected networks linking hundreds of millions of computers around the world. As such, the Internet is international, decentralized, and comprised of networks and infrastructure largely owned and operated by private sector entities. As the Internet grows and becomes more pervasive in all aspects of modern society, the question of how it should be governed becomes more pressing. This book reviews the issues, the management, and future of internet governance.

In: Internet Governance
Editor: Ernestine Saunders

ISBN: 978-1-63484-920-3

Chapter 1

INTERNET GOVERNANCE AND THE DOMAIN NAME SYSTEM: ISSUES FOR CONGRESS

Lennard G. Kruger

SUMMARY

The Internet is often described as a "network of networks" because it is not a single physical entity, but hundreds of thousands of interconnected networks linking hundreds of millions of computers around the world. As such, the Internet is international, decentralized, and comprised of networks and infrastructure largely owned and operated by private sector entities. As the Internet grows and becomes more pervasive in all aspects of modern society, the question of how it should be governed becomes more pressing.

Currently, an important aspect of the Internet is governed by a private sector, international organization called the Internet Corporation for Assigned Names and Numbers (ICANN), which manages and oversees some of the critical technical underpinnings of the Internet such as the domain name system and Internet Protocol (IP) addressing. ICANN makes its policy decisions using a multistakeholder model of governance, in which a "bottom-up" collaborative process is open to all constituencies of Internet stakeholders.

National governments have recognized an increasing stake in ICANN policy decisions, especially in cases where Internet policy intersects with national laws addressing such issues as intellectual property, privacy, law enforcement, and cybersecurity. Some governments around the world are advocating increased intergovernmental influence over the way the Internet is governed. For example, specific proposals have been advanced that would create an Internet governance entity within the United Nations (U.N.). Other governments (including the United States), as well as many other Internet stakeholders, oppose these proposals and argue that ICANN's multistakeholder model is the most appropriate way to govern the Internet.

Currently, the U.S. government, through the National Telecommunications and Information Administration (NTIA) at the Department of Commerce, holds a "stewardship" role over the domain name system by virtue of a contractual relationship with ICANN. On March 14, 2014, NTIA announced its intention to transition its stewardship role and procedural authority over key domain name functions to the global Internet multistakeholder community. If a satisfactory transition can be achieved, NTIA stated that it would let its contract with ICANN expire as early as September 30, 2015. On August 17, 2015, NTIA announced that the Internet Assigned Numbers Authority (IANA) contract will be extended for one year until September 30, 2016. NTIA has also stated that it will not accept any transition proposal that would replace the NTIA role with a government-led or an intergovernmental organization solution.

In the 114th Congress, H.R. 805/S. 1551 (the DOTCOM Act of 2015) would prohibit NTIA from relinquishing its authority until 30 legislative days after NTIA submits a report to Congress in which it certifies that the transition proposal meets certain criteria. On June 23, 2015, H.R. 805 was passed by the House. H.R. 2578 (FY2016 Commerce, Justice, Science (CJS) Appropriations Act), as passed by the House, directs that NTIA may not use any FY2016 appropriated funds to relinquish its responsibility with respect to Internet domain name system functions.

The 114th Congress is likely to closely examine NTIA's proposed transition of its authority. As a transition plan is developed by the Internet community, Congress will likely monitor and evaluate that plan, and seek assurances that an Internet and domain name system free of U.S. government stewardship will remain stable, secure, resilient, and open. Congress will likely continue assessing to what extent ongoing and future intergovernmental telecommunications conferences constitute an opportunity for some nations to increase intergovernmental control over the Internet, and how effectively the Administration is working to counteract that threat.

Meanwhile, in the wake of the November 13, 2015, terrorist attack in Paris, and with ongoing concern over the use of the Internet by terrorist organizations, the question has arisen whether Internet governance mechanisms could be used to combat the use of the Internet by terrorist entities. While nation-states can govern the use and content of the Internet within their own borders, there is no international governance entity that currently has authority to remove global Internet content used to promote terrorism.

WHAT IS INTERNET GOVERNANCE?

There is no universally agreed-upon definition of "Internet governance." A more limited definition would encompass the management and coordination of the technical underpinnings of the Internet—such as domain names, addresses, standards, and protocols that enable the Internet to function. A broader definition would include the many factors that shape a variety of Internet policy-related issues, such as such as intellectual property, privacy, Internet freedom, e-commerce, and cybersecurity.

One working definition was developed at the World Summit on the Information Society (WSIS) in 2005:

> Internet governance is the development and application by governments, the private sector and civil society, in their respective roles, of shared principles, norms, rules, decision-making procedures, and programmes that shape the evolution and use of the Internet.[1]

Another definition developed by the Internet Governance Project (IGP)[2] delineates three aspects of the Internet that may require some level of governing: *technical standardization*, which involves arriving at and agreeing upon technical standards and protocols; *resource allocation and assignment*, which includes domain names and Internet Protocol (IP) addresses; and *human conduct on the Internet*, encompassing the regulations, rules, and policies affecting areas such as spam, cybercrime, copyright and trademark disputes, consumer protection issues, and public and private security. With these three categories in mind, the IGP definition is:

> Internet governance is collective decisionmaking by owners, operators, developers, and users of the networks connected by Internet protocols to establish policies, rules, and dispute resolution procedures about technical standards, resource allocations, and/or the conduct of people engaged in global internetworking activities.[3]

How Is the Internet Currently Governed?

The nature of the Internet, with its decentralized architecture and structure, makes the practice of governing a complex proposition. First, the Internet is inherently international and cannot in its totality be governed by national governments whose authority ends at national borders. Second, the Internet's successful functioning depends on the willing cooperation and participation by mostly private sector stakeholders around the world. These stakeholders include owners and operators of servers and networks around the world, domain name registrars and registries, regional IP address allocation organizations, standards organizations, Internet service providers, and Internet users.

Given the multiplicity and diversity of Internet stakeholders, a number of organizations and entities play varying roles. It is important to note that all of the Internet stakeholders cited above participate in various ways within the various fora, organizations, and frameworks addressing Internet governance and policy.

Key organizations in the private sector include the following:

Internet Corporation for Assigned Names and Numbers (ICANN)—ICANN was created in 1998 through a Memorandum of Understanding with the Department of Commerce (see the following section of this report, "Role of U.S. Government"). Directed by an internationally constituted Board of Directors, ICANN is a private, not-for-profit organization based in Los Angeles, CA, which manages and oversees the critical technical underpinnings of the Internet such as the domain name system (DNS) and IP addressing (see the *Appendix* for more background information on ICANN). ICANN implements and enforces many of its policies and rules through contracts with *registries* (companies and organizations who operate and administer the master database of all domain names registered in each top level domain, such as .com and .org) and accredited *registrars* (the hundreds of companies and organizations with which consumers register domain names). Policies are developed by Supporting Organizations and Committees in a consensus-based "bottom-up" process open to various constituencies and stakeholders of the Internet. As such, ICANN is often pointed to as emblematic of the "multistakeholder model" of Internet governance.

Internet standards organizations—As the Internet has evolved, groups of engineers, researchers, users, and other interested parties have coalesced to develop technical standards and protocols necessary to enable the Internet to function smoothly. These organizations conduct standards development processes that are open to participants and volunteers from around the world. Internet standards organizations include the Internet Engineering Task Force (IETF), the Internet Architecture Board (IAB), the Internet Society (ISOC), and the World Wide Web Consortium (W3C).

Governmental entities involved in Internet governance include the following:

Governmental Advisory Committee (GAC) — As part of ICANN's multistakeholder process, the GAC provides advice to the ICANN Board on matters of public policy, especially in cases where ICANN activities and policies may interact with national laws or international agreements related to issues such as intellectual property, law enforcement, and privacy. GAC advice is developed through consensus among member nations. Although the ICANN Board is required to consider GAC advice and recommendations, it is not obligated to follow those recommendations. Membership in the GAC is open to all national governments who wish to participate. Currently, there are 146 members. The GAC Chair is currently held by Switzerland, with Vice Chairs held by Argentina, Spain, Namibia, Turkey, and Thailand.

Internet Governance Forum (IGF)—The IGF was established in 2006 by the United Nations' World Summit on the Information Society (WSIS). The purpose of the IGF is to provide a multistakeholder forum which provides an open discussion (in yearly meetings) on public policies related to the Internet. Open to all stakeholders and interested parties (governments, industry, academia, civil society), the IGF serves as an open discussion forum and does not have negotiated outcomes, nor does it make formal recommendations to the U.N. In December 2010, the U.N. General Assembly renewed the IGF through 2015 and tasked the U.N.'s Commission on Science and Technology for Development (CSTD) to develop a report and recommendations on how the IGF might be improved. A Working Group on Improvements to the Internet Governance Forum was formed by the U.N., which includes 22 governments (including the United States) and the participation of Internet stakeholder groups.

Other International Organizations — Other existing international organizations address Internet policy issues in various ways. The International Telecommunications Union (ITU) is the United Nations' specialized agency for communications and information technology. The World Intellectual Property Organization (WIPO) is another specialized agency of the U.N., which addresses a wide range of intellectual property issues, including those related to Internet policy. The Organisation for Economic Co-operation and Development (OECD) provides a forum for governments to work together to address economic issues, including the recent development of Internet policymaking principles. While none of these organizations have direct control or authority over the Internet, their activities can have influence over future directions of global Internet policy.

National governments — National governments have acted to address various Internet policy issues within their own borders. Many of the national laws and regulations pertain to user behavior on the Internet. For example, in the United States, laws have been passed addressing such issues as cybersecurity and cybercrime, Internet gambling, Internet privacy, and protection of intellectual property on the Internet. Governments have also established internal Internet policy coordinating bodies (e.g., the National Telecommunications and Information Administration's Internet Policy Task Force and the European Commission's Information Society).

ROLE OF U.S. GOVERNMENT

The U.S. government has no statutory authority over ICANN or the domain name system. However, because the Internet evolved from a network infrastructure created by the Department of Defense, the U.S. government originally owned and operated (primarily through private contractors) many of the key components of network architecture that enabled the domain name system to function. In the early 1990s, the National Science Foundation (NSF) was given a lead role in overseeing domain names used in the civilian portion of the Internet (which at that time was largely comprised of research universities). By the late 1990s, ICANN was created, the Internet had expanded into the commercial world, and the National Telecommunications and Information Administration (NTIA) of the Department of Commerce (DOC) assumed the lead role.

A 1998 Memorandum of Understanding between ICANN and the DOC initiated a process intended to transition technical DNS coordination and management functions to a private-sector not-for-profit entity. While the DOC plays no role in the internal governance or day-to-day operations of ICANN, the U.S. government, through the DOC/NTIA, retains a role with respect to the DNS via three separate contractual agreements. These are

- a 2009 Affirmation of Commitments (AoC) between DOC and ICANN;[4]
- a contract between ICANN and DOC to perform various technical functions such as allocating IP address blocks, editing the root zone file, and coordinating the assignment of unique protocol numbers; and
- a cooperative agreement between DOC and VeriSign to manage and maintain the official DNS root zone file.

By virtue of those three contractual agreements, the U.S. government—through DOC/NTIA— exerts a legacy authority and stewardship over ICANN, and arguably has more influence over ICANN and the DNS than other national governments.

While NTIA is the lead agency overseeing domain name issues, other federal agencies maintain a specific interest in the DNS that may affect their particular missions. For example, the Federal Trade Commission (FTC) seeks to protect consumer privacy on the Internet, the Department of Justice (DOJ) addresses Internet crime and intellectual property issues, and the Department of Defense and Department of Homeland Security address cybersecurity issues. However, none of these agencies has legal authority over ICANN or the running of the DNS.

Affirmation of Commitments

On September 30, 2009, DOC and ICANN announced agreement on an Affirmation of Commitments (AoC) to "institutionalize and memorialize" the technical coordination of the DNS globally and by a private-sector-led organization.[5] The AoC replaced the previous Memorandum of Understanding and subsequent Joint Project Agreement between DOC and ICANN. It has no expiration date and would conclude only if one of the two parties decided to terminate the agreement.

Under the AoC, ICANN committed to remain a not-for-profit corporation "headquartered in the United States of America with offices around the world to meet the needs of a global community." According to the AoC, "ICANN is a private organization and nothing in this Affirmation should be construed as control by any one entity." Specifically, the AoC called for the establishment of review panels which will periodically make recommendations to the ICANN Board in four areas: ensuring accountability, transparency, and the interests of global Internet users (panel includes the Administrator of NTIA);

preserving security, stability, and resiliency; impact of new generic top level domains (gTLDs); and WHOIS policy.[6]

On December 31, 2010, the Accountability and Transparency Review Team (ATRT) released its recommendations to the Board for improving ICANN's transparency and accountability with respect to Board governance and performance, the role and effectiveness of the GAC and its interaction with the Board, public input and policy development processes, and review mechanisms for Board decisions.[7] At the June 2011 meeting in Singapore, the Board adopted all 27 ATRT recommendations. According to NTIA, "the focus turns to ICANN management and staff, who must take up the challenge of implementing these recommendations as rapidly as possible and in a manner that leads to meaningful and lasting reform."[8]

DOC Contract and Cooperative Agreement with ICANN and VeriSign

A contract between DOC and ICANN—specifically referred to as the "IANA[9] functions contract"—authorizes ICANN to manage the technical underpinnings of the DNS. Specifically, the contract allows ICANN to perform various critical technical functions such as allocating IP address blocks, editing the root zone file, and coordinating the assignment of unique protocol numbers. Additionally, and intertwined with the IANA functions, a cooperative agreement between DOC and VeriSign (the company that operates the .com and .net registries) authorizes VeriSign to manage and maintain the official root zone file that is contained in the Internet's root servers that underlie the functioning of the DNS.[10] By virtue of these legal agreements, the DOC approves changes or modifications made to the root zone file (changes, for example, such as adding a new top level domain).[11]

On July 2, 2012, NTIA announced the award of the most recent (and current) IANA contract to ICANN through September 30, 2015 (with an option to extend the contract through September 2019). The IANA contract continues to specify that the contractor must be a wholly U.S. owned and operated firm or a U.S. university or college; that all primary operations and systems shall remain within the United States; and that the U.S. government reserves the right to inspect the premises, systems, and processes of all facilities and components used for the performance of the contract.

NTIA Intent to Transition Stewardship of the DNS[12]

The IANA functions contract with ICANN and the cooperative agreement with Verisign give NTIA the authority to maintain a stewardship and oversight role with respect to ICANN and the domain name system. On March 14, 2014, NTIA announced its intention to transition its stewardship role and procedural authority over key domain name functions to the global Internet multistakeholder community.[13] NTIA's stated intention was that it would let its IANA functions contract with ICANN expire on September 30, 2015, if a satisfactory transition could be achieved. With NTIA having the option of extending the contract for up to two two-year periods through September 30, 2019, NTIA announced on August 17, 2015, that it will extend the IANA functions contract through September 30, 2016.

NTIA asked ICANN to convene interested global Internet stakeholders (both from the private sector and governments) to develop a proposal to achieve the transition. Specifically, NTIA expects ICANN to work collaboratively with parties directly affected by the IANA contract, including the Internet Engineering Task Force (IETF), the Internet Architecture Board (IAB), the Internet Society (ISOC), the Regional Internet Registries (RIRs), top level domain name operators, Verisign, and other interested global stakeholders. In October 2013, many of these groups—specifically, the Internet technical organizations responsible for coordination of the Internet infrastructure—had called for "accelerating the globalization of ICANN and IANA functions, towards an environment in which all stakeholders, including all governments, participate on an equal footing."[14]

NTIA has stated that it will not accept any transition proposal that would replace the NTIA role with a government-led or an intergovernmental organization solution.

In addition, NTIA told ICANN that the transition proposal must have broad community support and address the following four principles:

- support and enhance the multistakeholder model;
- maintain the security, stability, and resilience of the Internet DNS;
- meet the needs and expectation of the global customers and partners of the IANA services; and
- maintain the openness of the Internet.

Supporters of the transition[15] argue that by transferring its remaining authority over ICANN and the DNS to the global Internet community, the U.S.

government will bolster its continuing support for the multistakeholder model of Internet governance, and that this will enable the United States to more effectively argue and work against proposals for intergovernmental control over the Internet. Supporters also point out that the U.S. government and Internet stakeholders have, from the inception of ICANN, envisioned that U.S. authority over IANA functions would be temporary, and that the DNS would eventually be completely privatized.[16] According to NTIA, this transition is now possible, given that "ICANN as an organization has matured and taken steps in recent years to improve its accountability and transparency and its technical competence."[17]

Those opposed, skeptical, or highly cautious about the transition[18] point out that NTIA's role has served as a necessary "backstop" which has given Internet stakeholders confidence that the integrity and stability of the DNS is being sufficiently overseen. Critics assert that in the wake of the Edward Snowden NSA revelations, foreign governments might gain more support internationally in their continuing attempts to exert intergovernmental control over the Internet, and that any added intergovernmental influence over the Internet and the DNS would be that much more detrimental to the interests of the United States if NTIA's authority over ICANN and the DNS were to no longer exist. Another concern regards the development of the transition plan and a new international multistakeholder entity that would provide some level of stewardship over the domain name system. Critics are concerned about the risks of foreign governments— particularly those favoring censorship of the Internet—gaining influence over the DNS through the transition to a new Internet governance mechanism that no longer is subject to U.S. government oversight.

Multistakeholder Process to Develop a Transition Proposal

ICANN has convened a process through which the multistakeholder community will attempt to come to consensus on a transition proposal. The process is divided into two separate but related parallel tracks: (1) IANA Stewardship Transition and (2) Enhancing ICANN Accountability.

Legislative Activities in the 113th Congress

On March 27, 2014, Representative Shimkus introduced H.R. 4342, the Domain Openness Through Continued Oversight Matters (DOTCOM) Act. H.R. 4342 would have prohibited the NTIA from relinquishing responsibility over the Internet domain name system until GAO submits to Congress a report on the role of the NTIA with respect to such system. The report would have included a discussion and analysis of the advantages and disadvantages of the change and address the national security concerns raised by relinquishing U.S. oversight. It would also have required GAO to provide a definition of the term "multistakeholder model" as used by NTIA with respect to Internet policymaking and governance. H.R. 4342 was referred to the House Energy and Commerce Committee. On April 2, 2014, the Subcommittee on Communications and Technology held a hearing on the DOTCOM Act.[19] H.R. 4342 was approved by the House Energy and Commerce Committee on May 8, 2014. Subsequently on June 5, 2014, the House Energy and Commerce Committee requested that the GAO examine the Administration's proposal to transition NTIA's current authority over IANA to the multistakeholder Internet community.[20]

On May 22, 2014, the text of the DOTCOM Act was offered by Representative Shimkus as an amendment to H.R. 4435, the National Defense Authorization Act for FY2015. During House consideration of H.R. 4435, the amendment was agreed to by a vote of 245-177. H.R. 4435 was passed by the House on May 22, 2014. The House Armed Services bill report accompanying H.R. 4435 (H.Rept. 113-446) stated the committee's belief that any new Internet governance structure should include protections for the Department of Defense-controlled .mil generic top level domain and its associated Internet protocol numbers. The committee also supported maintaining separation between the policymaking and technical operation of root-zone management functions.

On June 2, 2014, the Senate Armed Services Committee reported S. 2410, its version of the FY2015 National Defense Authorization Act. Section 1646 of S. 2410 ("Sense of Congress on the Future of the Internet and the .mil Top-Level Domain") stated that it is the sense of Congress that the Secretary of Defense should

> advise the President to transfer the remaining role of the United States Government in the functions of the Internet Assigned Numbers Authority to a global multi-stakeholder community only if the President is confident that the '.MIL' top-level domain and the Internet Protocol address numbers used exclusively by the Department of Defense for national security will remain exclusively used by the Department of Defense.

Section 1646 also directed DOD to take "all necessary steps to sustain the successful stewardship and good standing of the Internet root zone servers managed by components of the Department of Defense." In the report accompanying S. 2410 (S.Rept. 113-176), the committee urged DOD to

> seek an agreement through the IANA transition process, or in parallel to it, between the United States and the Internet Corporation for Assigned Names and Numbers and the rest of the global Internet stakeholders that the .mil domain will continue to be afforded the same generic top level domain status after the transition that it has always enjoyed, on a par with all other country-specific domains.

The Carl Levin and Howard P. "Buck" McKeon National Defense Authorization Act for Fiscal Year 2015 was signed by the President on December 16, 2014 (P.L. 113-235). The enacted law does not contain the DOTCOM Act provision contained in the House-passed version. Section 1639 of P.L. 113-235 ("Sense of Congress on the Future of the Internet and the .mil Top-Level Domain") states it is the sense of Congress that the Secretary of Defense should support the IANA transfer

> only if assurances are provided for the protection of the current status of legacy top-level domain names and Internet Protocol address numbers, particularly those used by the Department of Defense and the components of the U.S. Government for national security purposes; mechanisms are institutionalized to uphold and protect consensus-based decision making in the multi-stakeholder approach; and existing stress-testing scenarios of the accountability process of the multi-stakeholder model can be confidently shown to work transparently, securely, and efficiently to maintain a free, open, and resilient Internet.

It is also the sense of Congress that the Secretary of Defense should "take all necessary steps to sustain the successful stewardship and good standing of the Internet root zone servers managed by components of the Department of Defense, including active participation, review, and analysis for transition planning documents and accountability stress testing."

On May 8, 2014, the House Appropriations Committee approved H.R. 4660, the FY2015 Commerce, Justice, Science (CJS) Appropriations Act, which appropriates funds for DOC and NTIA. The bill report (H.Rept. 113-448) stated that in order that the transition be more fully considered by Congress, the committee's recommendation for NTIA does not include any funds to carry out the transition and that the committee expects that NTIA will maintain the existing no-cost contract with ICANN throughout FY2015.

During House consideration of H.R. 4660, an amendment offered by Representative Duffy was adopted on May 30, 2014 (by recorded vote, 229-178), which stated that (Section 562) "[n]one of the funds made available by this Act may be used to relinquish the responsibility of the National Telecommunications and Information Administration with respect to Internet domain name system functions, including responsibility with respect to the authoritative root zone file and the Internet Assigned Numbers Authority functions." H.R. 4660 was subsequently passed by the House on May 30, 2014.

On June 5, 2014, the Senate Appropriations Committee reported its version of the FY2015 Commerce, Justice, Science, and Related Agencies Appropriations Act (S. 2437). In the bill report (S.Rept. 113-181) the committee directed NTIA to conduct a thorough review and analysis of any proposed transition of the IANA contract in order to ensure that ICANN has in place an NTIA approved multi-stakeholder oversight plan that is insulated from foreign government and intergovernmental control. Further, the committee directed NTIA to report quarterly to the committee on all aspects of the privatization process and further directed NTIA to inform the committee, as well as the Committee on Commerce, Science, and Transportation, not less than seven days in advance of any decision with respect to a successor contract. The committee also expressed its concern that NTIA has not been a strong advocate for U.S. businesses and consumers through its participation in ICANN's Governmental Advisory Committee (GAC), and stated that it awaits "the past due report on NTIA's plans for greater involvement in the GAC and the efforts it is undertaking to protect U.S. consumers, companies, and intellectual property."

The Consolidated and Further Continuing Appropriations Act, 2015 (P.L. 113-235) was signed by the President on December 16, 2014. Section 540 provides that during FY2015, NTIA may not use any appropriated funds to relinquish its responsibility with respect to Internet domain name system functions, including its responsibility with respect to the authoritative root zone file and the IANA functions. The prohibition on funding for NTIA's IANA transition activities expires on September 30, 2015. Additionally, the Explanatory Statement accompanying P.L. 113-235 reiterates House and Senate language regarding ICANN and IANA matters and modifies the Senate language by directing NTIA "to inform appropriate Congressional committees not less than 45 days in advance of any such proposed successor contract or any other decision related to changing NTIA's role with respect to ICANN or IANA activities." The Explanatory Statement also directs NTIA to submit a report to the House and Senate Committees on Appropriations within 45 days of enactment of P.L. 113-235 regarding "any recourse that would be available to the United States if the decision is made to transition to a new contract and any subsequent decisions made following such transfer of Internet governance are deleterious to the United States."

Other legislation addressing the proposed transition included the following:

- H.R. 4367 (Internet Stewardship Act of 2014, introduced by Representative Mike Kelly on April 2, 2014), which would have prohibited NTIA from relinquishing its DNS responsibilities unless permitted by statute;
- H.R. 4398 (Global Internet Freedom Act of 2014, introduced by Representative Duffy on April 4, 2014), which would have prohibited NTIA from relinquishing its authority over the IANA functions; and
- H.R. 5737 (Defending Internet Freedom Act of 2014, introduced by Representative Mike Kelly on November 19, 2014), which would have prohibited NTIA from relinquishing its responsibilities over domain name functions unless it certifies that the transition proposal meets certain specified criteria.

H.R. 4367, H.R. 4398, and H.R. 5737 were referred to the Committee on Energy and Commerce. Meanwhile, the House Judiciary Committee, Subcommittee on Courts, Intellectual Property, and the Internet, held a hearing on April 10, 2014, that examined the proposed transition.

Legislative Activities in the 114th Congress

House Legislation

The DOTCOM Act of the 113th Congress was reintroduced into the 114th Congress by Representative Shimkus as H.R. 805 on February 5, 2015. As introduced, the DOTCOM Act of 2015 would have prohibited NTIA from relinquishing responsibility over the Internet domain name system until GAO submitted a report to Congress examining the implications of the proposed transfer. H.R. 805 would have directed GAO to issue the report no later than one year after NTIA received a transition proposal. On June 17, 2015, the House Committee on Energy and Commerce approved an amended DOTCOM Act. The amended version of H.R. 805 reflected a bipartisan agreement and was approved unanimously by voice vote. On June 23, 2015, H.R. 805 was passed by the House (378-25) under suspension of the rules.

H.R. 805, as passed by the House, does not permit NTIA's authority over the IANA function "to terminate, lapse, be cancelled, or otherwise cease to be in effect" until 30 legislative days after NTIA submits a report to Congress on the final IANA transition proposal. Specifically, the report must contain the final transition proposal and a certification by NTIA that the proposal

- supports and enhances the multistakeholder model of Internet governance;
- maintains the security, stability, and resiliency of the Internet domain name system;
- meets the needs and expectations of the global customers and partners of IANA services;
- maintains the openness of the Internet; and
- does not replace the role of NTIA with a government-led or intergovernmental organization solution.

H.R. 805 also requires NTIA to certify that the required changes to ICANN's bylaws contained in the transition proposal have been adopted by ICANN.

Meanwhile, on June 3, 2015, the House passed H.R. 2578, the FY2016 Commerce, Justice, Science (CJS) Appropriations Act, which appropriates funds for DOC and NTIA. Section 536 of H.R. 2578 states that "[n]one of the funds made available by this Act may be used to relinquish the responsibility of the National Telecommunications and Information Administration with respect to Internet domain name system functions, including responsibility with respect to the authoritative root zone file and the Internet Assigned Numbers Authority functions."

Other House-introduced legislation that addresses the proposed IANA transition includes:

- H.R. 355 (Global Internet Freedom Act of 2015, introduced by Representative Duffy on January 14, 2015), which would prohibit NTIA from relinquishing its authority over the IANA functions.
- H.R. 2251 (Defending Internet Freedom Act of 2015, introduced by Representative Mike Kelly on May 15, 2015), which would prohibit NTIA from relinquishing its responsibilities over domain name

functions and the IANA function unless it certifies that the transition proposal meets certain specified criteria.

Senate Legislation

S. 1551, the Senate companion version of the DOTCOM Act of 2015, was introduced on June 11, 2015, by Senator Thune. The language of S. 1551 is virtually identical to H.R. 805 as approved by the House Committee on Energy and Commerce. S. 1551 was referred to the Senate Committee on Commerce, Science, and Transportation and was ordered to be reported by the committee on June 25, 2015.

On June 16, 2015, the Senate Appropriations Committee reported its version of the FY2016 Commerce, Justice, Science, and Related Agencies Appropriations Act. In the bill report (S.Rept. 114-66) the committee directed NTIA to

> continue quarterly reports to the Committee on all aspects of the transition process, and further directs NTIA to inform the Committee and the Senate Committee on Commerce, Science and Transportation, not less than 45 days in advance of any decision with respect to a successor contract." The committee also stated that it "continues to be concerned about this process and supports the continued stewardship role of the United States over the domain name system in order to ensure the security of the .gov and .mil domains and to protect the freedom of speech and expression internationally.

Also in the Senate, S.Res. 71—designating the week of February 8 through February 14, 2015, as "Internet Governance Awareness Week"—was introduced by Senator Hatch on February 5, 2015. S.Res. 71 seeks to increase public awareness regarding NTIA's proposed transition, encourage public education about the importance of the transition process; and call the attention of the participants at the ICANN meeting in Singapore to the importance of designing accountability and governance reforms to best prepare ICANN for executing the responsibilities that it may receive under any transition of the stewardship of the IANA functions. S.Res. 71 was passed by the Senate on February 5, 2015.

Congressional Hearings

As part of its continuing oversight over NTIA and the domain name system, Congress has held hearings on the proposed IANA transition and on ICANN's management of the domain name system:

- On February 25, 2015, the Senate Committee on Commerce, Science, and Transportation held a hearing entitled, "Preserving the Multistakeholder Model of Internet Governance."[21]
- On May 13, 2015, the House Committee on Energy and Commerce, Subcommittee on Communications and Technology, held a hearing entitled, "Stakeholder Perspectives on the IANA Transition."[22]
- On May 13, 2015, the House Committee on the Judiciary, Subcommittee on Courts, Intellectual Property and the Internet, held a hearing entitled, "Stakeholder Perspectives on ICANN: the .Sucks Domain and Essential Steps to Guarantee Trust and Accountability in the Internet's Operation."23
- On July 8, 2015, the House Committee on Energy and Commerce, Subcommittee on Communications and Technology, held a hearing entitled, "Internet Governance Progress After ICANN 53."[24]

Other Activities

On September 22, 2015, the Chairmen of the House and Senate Judiciary Committees (Representatives Goodlatte and Senator Grassley), Senator Cruz, and Representative Issa sent a letter to GAO expressing concern that the IANA transition and the relinquishing of U.S. government control over the root zone file may constitute a transfer of government property that may only be authorized by an act of Congress.[25] Specifically, the letter asked GAO to examine three questions: would the termination of NTIA's contract with ICANN cause government property of any kind to be transferred to ICANN; is the root zone file or other related or similar materials or information U.S. government property; and if so, does NTIA have the authority to transfer the root zone file or other related materials or information to a nonfederal entity?

On October 15, 2015, the Chairman of the Senate Committee on Commerce, Science, and Transportation and the Ranking Member of the Subcommittee on Communications, Technology, Innovation, and the Internet (Senator Thune and Senator Schatz) sent a letter[26] to ICANN calling for robust accountability reforms which may lessen the Board's power and authority if those reforms conform with the multistakeholder community's accountability proposal. The Senators further stated that no arbitrary deadlines should be used as a way to deter the community from securing the reforms it must have to sufficiently replace the role currently played by NTIA.

DEBATE OVER FUTURE MODEL OF INTERNET GOVERNANCE

Given its complexity, diversity, and international nature, how should the Internet be governed? Some assert that a multistakeholder model of governance is appropriate, where all stakeholders (both public and private sectors) arrive at consensus through a transparent bottom-up process. Others argue that a greater role for national governments is necessary, either through increased influence through the multistakeholder model, or under the auspices of an international body exerting intergovernmental control.

To date, ICANN and the governance of the domain name system has been the focal point of this debate. While ICANN's mandate is to manage portions of the technical infrastructure of the Internet (domain names and IP addresses), many of the decisions ICANN makes affect other aspects of Internet policy, including areas such as intellectual property, privacy, and cybersecurity. These are areas which many national governments have addressed for their own citizens and constituencies through domestic legislation, as well as through international treaties.

As part of the debate over an appropriate model of Internet governance, criticisms of ICANN have arisen on two fronts. One criticism reflects the tension between national governments and the current performance and governance processes of ICANN, whereby governments feel they lack adequate influence over ICANN decisions that affect a range of Internet policy issues. The other criticism is fueled by concerns of many nations that the U.S. government holds undue legacy influence and control over ICANN and the domain name system.

The debate over multistakeholderism vs. intergovernmental control initially manifested itself in 2005 at the World Summit on the Information Society (WSIS), which was a conference organized by the United Nations. More recently, this debate has been rekindled in various international fora, partially sparked by two ICANN actions in 2011: the approval of the .xxx top-level domain and the approval of a process to allow an indefinite number of new generic top level domains (gTLDs).

2005 World Summit on the Information Society (WSIS)

Following the creation of ICANN in 1998, many in the international community, including foreign governments, argued that it was inappropriate for the U.S. government to maintain its legacy authority over ICANN and the DNS. They suggested that management of the DNS should be accountable to a higher intergovernmental body. The United Nations, at the first phase of the WSIS in December 2003, debated and agreed to study the issue of how to achieve greater international involvement in the governance of the Internet, and the domain name system in particular. The study was conducted by the U.N.'s Working Group on Internet Governance (WGIG). On July 14, 2005, the WGIG released its report,[27] stating that no single government should have a preeminent role in relation to international Internet governance. The report called for further internationalization of Internet governance, and proposed the creation of a new global forum for Internet stakeholders. Four possible models were put forth, including two involving the creation of new Internet governance bodies linked to the U.N. Under three of the four models, ICANN would either be supplanted or made accountable to a higher intergovernmental body. The report's conclusions were scheduled to be considered during the second phase of the WSIS held in Tunis in November 2005. U.S. officials stated their opposition to transferring control and administration of the domain name system from ICANN to any international body. Similarly, the 109th Congress expressed its support for maintaining existing U.S. control over ICANN and the DNS (H.Con.Res. 268 and S.Res. 323).[28]

The European Union (EU) initially supported the U.S. position. However, during the September 2005 preparatory meetings, the EU seemingly shifted its support towards an approach which favored an enhanced international role in governing the Internet. Conflict at the WSIS Tunis Summit over control of the domain name system was averted by the announcement, on November 15, 2005, of an Internet governance agreement between the United States, the EU, and over 100 other nations. Under this agreement, ICANN and the United States maintained their roles with respect to the domain name system. A new international group under the auspices of the U.N. was formed—the Internet Governance Forum (IGF)—which would provide an ongoing forum for all stakeholders (both governments and nongovernmental groups) to discuss and debate Internet policy issues.

Creation of the .xxx Domain and New gTLDs

Starting in 2010 and 2011, controversies surrounding the roll-out of new generic top level domains (gTLDs) and the addition of the .xxx TLD led some governments to argue for increased government influence on the ICANN policy development process.[29]

.xxx

Since 2000, ICANN has repeatedly considered whether to allow the establishment of a gTLD for adult content. On June 1, 2005, ICANN announced that it had entered into commercial and technical negotiations with a registry company (ICM Registry) to operate a new ".xxx" domain, which would be designated for use by adult websites. With the ICANN Board scheduled to consider final approval of the .xxx domain on August 16, 2005, the Department of Commerce sent a letter to ICANN requesting that adequate additional time be provided to allow ICANN to address the objections of individuals expressing concerns about the impact of pornography on families and children and opposing the creation of a new top level domain devoted to adult content. ICANN's Governmental Advisory Committee (GAC) also requested more time before the final decision.

On March 30, 2007, the ICANN Board voted 9-5 to deny the .xxx domain. ICM Registry subsequently challenged ICANN's decision before an Independent Review Panel (IRP), claiming that ICANN's rejection of ICM's application for a .xxx gTLD was not consistent with ICANN's Articles of Incorporation and Bylaws. On February 19, 2010, a three-person Independent Review Panel ruled primarily in favor of ICM Registry, finding that its application for the .xxx TLD had met the required criteria.

Subsequently, on June 25, 2010, at the ICANN meeting in Brussels, the Board of Directors voted to allow ICM's .xxx application to move forward, and at the December 2010 ICANN meeting, the ICANN Board passed a resolution stating that while "it intends to enter into a registry agreement with ICM Registry for the .xxx TLD," the Board would enter into a formal consultation with the Governmental Advisory Committee on areas where the Board's decision was in conflict with GAC advice relating to the ICM application.[30]

While not officially or formally in opposition to the approval of .xxx, the GAC advised ICANN that "there is no active support of the GAC for the introduction of a .xxx TLD" and that "while there are members, which neither endorse nor oppose the introduction of a .xxx TLD, others are emphatically opposed from a public policy perspective to the introduction of an .xxx

TLD."[31] The GAC listed a number of specific issues and objections that it wished ICANN to resolve.

A February 2011 letter from ICANN to the GAC acknowledged and responded to areas where approving the .xxx registry agreement with ICM would conflict with GAC advice received by ICANN.[32] The Board acknowledged that ICANN and the GAC were not able to reach a mutually acceptable solution, and ultimately, on March 18, 2011, the Board approved a resolution giving the CEO or General Counsel of ICANN the authority to execute the registry agreement with ICM to establish a .xxx TLD. The vote was nine in favor, three opposed, and four abstentions.

The decision to create a .xxx TLD was not viewed favorably by many governments.[33] In an April 6, 2011, letter to the Department of Commerce, the European Commissioner for the Digital Agenda asked that the introduction of .xxx be delayed.[34] In its response, NTIA said it "share[s] your disappointment that ICANN ignored the clear advice of governments worldwide, including the United States, by approving the new .xxx domain."[35] However, NTIA stated why it would not (and did not) interfere with the addition of .xxx:

> While the Obama Administration does not support ICANN's decision, we respect the multi-stakeholder Internet governance process and do not think that it is in the long-term best interest of the United States or the global Internet community for us unilaterally to reverse the decision. Our goal is to preserve the global Internet, which is a force for innovation, economic growth, and the free flow of information. I agree with you that the Board took its action without the full support of the community and accordingly, I am dedicated to improving the responsiveness of ICANN to all stakeholders, including governments worldwide.[36]

gTLD Expansion

Top Level Domains (TLDs) are the suffixes that appear at the end of an address (after the "dot"). Prior to ICANN's establishment in 1998, the Internet had eight generic top level domains (gTLDs), including .com, .org, .net, and .gov. In 2000 and 2004, ICANN held application rounds for a limited number of new gTLDs—currently there are 22. Some are reserved or restricted to particular types of organizations (e.g., .museum, .gov, .travel) and others are open for registration by anyone (.com, .org, .info). Applicants for new gTLDs are typically commercial entities and nonprofit organizations who seek to become ICANN-recognized registries that will establish and operate name servers for their TLD registry, as well as implement a domain name registration process for that particular TLD.

The growth of the Internet and the accompanying growth in demand for domain names have focused the debate on whether and how to further expand the number of gTLDs. Beginning in 2005, ICANN embarked on a long consultative process to develop rules and procedures for introducing and adopting an indefinite number of new gTLDs into the domain name system. A new gTLD can be any word or string of characters that is applied for and approved by ICANN. Between 2008 and 2011, ICANN released seven iterations of its gTLD Applicant Guidebook (essentially the rulebook for how the new gTLD program will be implemented). On June 20, 2011, the ICANN Board of Directors voted to approve the launch of the new gTLD program, under which potentially hundreds of new gTLDs could ultimately be approved by ICANN and introduced into the DNS. Applications for new gTLDs were to be accepted from January 12 through April 12, 2012.

The rollout of new gTLDs was controversial. Advocates (including the domain name industry) argued that a gTLD expansion will provide opportunities for Internet innovation and competition. On the other hand, many trademark holders pointed to possible higher costs and greater difficulties in protecting their trademarks across hundreds of new gTLDs. Similarly, governments expressed concern over intellectual property protections, and along with law enforcement entities, also cited concerns over the added burden of combating various cybercrimes (such as phishing and identity theft) across hundreds of new gTLDs. Throughout ICANN's policy development process, governments, through the Governmental Advisory Committee, advocated for additional intellectual property protections in the new gTLD process. The GAC also argued for more stringent rules that would allow for better law enforcement in the new domain space to better protect consumers. Although changes were made, strong opposition from many trademark holders[37] led to opposition from some parts of the U.S. government towards the end of 2011. For example:

- On December 8, 2011, the Senate Committee on Commerce, Science and Transportation held a hearing on the ICANN's expansion of TLDs. Subsequently, on December 28, 2011, a letter from Senator John Rockefeller, chairman of the Senate Committee on Commerce, Science and Transportation, to the Secretary of Commerce and the Administrator of NTIA, stated his concern that "this expansion of gTLDs, if it proceeds as planned, will have adverse consequences for the millions of American consumers, companies, and non-profit organizations that use the Internet on a daily basis" and that at the hearing, "witnesses speaking on behalf of more than a hundred companies and non-profit organizations explained that ICANN's current plan for gTLD expansion will likely cause millions of dollars in increased costs related to combating cybersquatting." In the letter, Senator Rockefeller requested that NTIA "should consider asking ICANN to either delay the opening of the application period or to drastically limit the number of new gTLDs it approves next year."[38] A subsequent December 22, 2011, letter to ICANN from Senators Klobuchar and Ayotte also registered concern over the TLD expansion and asked ICANN to further address law enforcement, trademark, and consumer concerns before launching the program.[39]

- On December 14, 2011, the House Committee on Energy and Commerce, Subcommittee on Communications and Technology, held a hearing on ICANN's top level domain program. Subsequently on December 21, 2011, a bipartisan group of committee members sent a letter to ICANN requesting that the expansion of the gTLDs be delayed, noting that "many stakeholders are not convinced that ICANN's process has resulted in an acceptable level of protection."[40] The Energy and Commerce Committee members argued that "a short delay will allow interested parties to work with ICANN and offer changes to alleviate many of them, specifically concerns over law enforcement, cost and transparency that were discussed in recent Congressional hearings."[41]
- A December 16, 2011, letter to the Secretary of Commerce from Representative Bob Goodlatte, chairman of the House Subcommittee on Intellectual Property, Competition, and the Internet, and Representative Howard Berman, ranking Member of the House Committee on Foreign Affairs, urged DOC to take all steps necessary to encourage ICANN to undertake further evaluation and review before the gTLD expansion is permitted to occur. The letter asked DOC to determine whether the benefits of the expansion outweigh the costs and risks to consumers, businesses, and the Internet, and that if the program proceeds, that ICANN should initially limit the expansion to a small pilot project which can be evaluated.[42] Previously, the Subcommittee on Intellectual Property, Competition, and the Internet had held a May 4, 2011, hearing on oversight of the gTLD program.

- A December 16, 2011, letter from the Federal Trade Commission (FTC) to ICANN argued that a "rapid, exponential expansion of gTLDs has the potential to magnify both the abuse of the domain name system and the corresponding challenges we encounter in tracking down Internet fraudsters." The FTC urged ICANN to implement the new gTLD program as a pilot program and substantially reduce the number of gTLDs that are introduced in the first application round, strengthen ICANN's contractual compliance program, develop a new ongoing program to monitor consumer issues that arise during the first round of implementing the new gTLD program, conduct an assessment of each new proposed gTLD's risk of consumer harm as part of the evaluation and approval process, and improve the accuracy of WHOIS data, including by imposing a registrant verification requirement. The FTC added that "ICANN should address these issues before it approves any new gTLD applications. If ICANN fails to address these issues responsibly, the introduction of new gTLDs could pose a significant threat to consumers and undermine consumer confidence in the Internet."[43]
- A December 27, 2011, letter to ICANN from the Senate and House Judiciary Committees expressed concerns over the new gTLD program and urged ICANN to "strengthen protections for consumers and trademark holders who risk being harmed by the proliferation of domain names on the web." The letter also urged ICANN to work closely with the law enforcement community "to ensure that the program's rollout does not adversely impact their efforts to fight fraud and abuse on the Internet."[44]

At the December 2011 House and Senate hearings, ICANN stated its intention to proceed with the gTLD expansion as planned. ICANN defended its gTLD program, arguing that the new gTLDs will offer more protections for consumers and trademark holders than current gTLDs; that new gTLDs will provide needed competition, choice, and innovation to the domain name system; and that critics have already had ample opportunity to contribute input during a seven-year deliberative policy development process.[45] Ultimately, ICANN did not delay the initiation of the new gTLD program, and the application window was opened on January 12, 2012, as planned.

Much of the pressure on ICANN to delay the new gTLD program was directed at NTIA, given NTIA's unique relationship with ICANN. At both the December 2011 Senate and House hearings, NTIA expressed support for

ICANN's planned rollout of the TLD expansion program, arguing that national governments have been able to address intellectual property, law enforcement, and consumer concerns through the Governmental Advisory Committee (GAC):

> NTIA believes that ICANN improved the new gTLD program by incorporating a significant number of proposals from the GAC. ICANN's new gTLD program also now provides law enforcement and consumer protection authorities with significantly more tools than those available in existing gTLDs to address malicious conduct. The fact that not all of the GAC's proposals were adopted as originally offered does not represent a failure of the process or a setback to governments; rather, it reflects the reality of a multi-stakeholder model.[46]

While NTIA stated that it would continue to monitor progress and push for necessary changes to ICANN's TLD expansion program, a key aspect of NTIA's argument for supporting ICANN's planned rollout was to preserve the integrity of the multistakeholder Internet governance process:

> NTIA is dedicated to maintaining an open, global Internet that remains a valuable tool for economic growth, innovation, and the free flow of information, goods, and services online. We believe the best way to achieve this goal is to continue to actively support and participate in multi-stakeholder Internet governance processes such as ICANN. This is in stark contrast to some countries that are actively seeking to move Internet policy to the United Nations. If we are to combat the proposals put forward by others, we need to ensure that our multi-stakeholder institutions have provided a meaningful role for governments as stakeholders. NTIA believes that the strength of the multi-stakeholder approach to Internet policy-making is that it allows for speed, flexibility, and decentralized problem-solving and stands in stark contrast to a more traditional, top-down regulatory model characterized by rigid processes, political capture by incumbents, and in so many cases, impasse or stalemate.[47]

On January 3, 2012, NTIA sent ICANN a letter concerning implementation of the new gTLD program.[48] While NTIA recognized that the program "is the product of a six-year international multistakeholder process" and that NTIA does "not seek to interfere with the decisions and compromises reached during that process," NTIA urged ICANN to consider implementing measures to address many of the criticisms raised. Such measures would address concerns of trademark holders, law enforcement, and consumer protection. NTIA also asked ICANN to assess (after the initial application window closes and the list of prospective new gTLDs is known) whether there is a need to phase in the introduction of new gTLDs, and whether additional trademark protection measures need to be taken.

NTIA concluded its letter as follows:

> How ICANN handles the new gTLD program will, for many, be a litmus test of the viability of this approach. For its part, NTIA is committed to continuing to be an active member of the GAC and working with stakeholders to mitigate any unintended consequences of the new gTLD program.[49]

As the new gTLDs go "live," many stakeholders are concerned that various forms of domain name abuse (e.g., trademark infringement, consumer fraud, malicious behavior, etc.) could manifest itself within the hundreds of new gTLD domain spaces. Thus, the effectiveness of ICANN's approach to addressing such issues as intellectual property protection of second level domain names and mitigating unlawful behavior in the domain name space will be of interest as the new gTLD program goes forward.

With respect to the new gTLD program, the GAC provided advice to the ICANN Board on any first round applications the GAC considered problematic. GAC advice can take three forms:

I. The GAC advises ICANN that it is the consensus of the GAC that a particular application should not proceed. This will create a strong presumption for the ICANN Board that the application should not be approved.

II. The GAC advises ICANN that there are concerns about a particular application "dot-example." The ICANN Board is expected to enter into dialogue with the GAC to understand the scope of concerns. The ICANN Board is also expected to provide a rationale for its decision.

III. The GAC advises ICANN that an application should not proceed unless remediated. This will raise a strong presumption for the Board that the application should not proceed unless there is a remediation method available in the Guidebook (such as securing the approval of one or more governments), that is implemented by the applicant.[50]

The GAC also issued Early Warnings to the ICANN Board in the event that any GAC member found an application problematic for any reason. An Early Warning was an indication that a formal GAC objection was possible (either through the GAC advice process or through the formal objection process). Applicants were notified of an Early Warning against their application and given the opportunity to address the concerns or to withdraw the application (thereby qualifying for a partial refund of the application fee).

Proposed Models for Internet Governance

As discussed above, ICANN is a working example of a multistakeholder model of Internet governance, whereby a bottom-up collaborative process is used to provide Internet stakeholders with access to the policymaking process. Support for the multistakeholder model of Internet governance is reflected in international organizations such as the Organisation for Economic Cooperation and Development (OECD) and the Group of Eight (G8). For example, the OECD's *Communiqué on Principles for Internet Policy-Making* cites multistakeholderism as a central tenet of Internet governance:

> In particular, continued support is needed for the multi-stakeholder environment, which has underpinned the process of Internet governance and the management of critical Internet resources (such as naming and numbering resources) and these various stakeholders should continue to fully play a role in this framework. Governments should also work in multi-stakeholder environments to achieve international public policy goals and strengthen international co-operation in Internet governance.[51]

Similarly, at the G8 Summit of Deauville on May 26-27, 2011, the G8 issued a declaration on its renewed commitment for freedom and democracy that contained a new section on the Internet. Support for a multistakeholder model for Internet governance with a significant national government role was made explicit:

> As we support the multi-stakeholder model of Internet governance, we call upon all stakeholders to contribute to enhanced cooperation within and between all international fora dealing with the governance of the Internet. In this regard, flexibility and transparency have to be maintained in order to adapt to the fast pace of technological and business

developments and uses. Governments have a key role to play in this model.[52]

As discussed above, in 2005, the World Summit on the Information Society (WSIS) considered four models of Internet governance, of which three would have involved an intergovernmental body to oversee the Internet and the domain name system. While the WSIS ultimately decided not to pursue an intergovernmental model in 2005, some nations have again advocated an intergovernmental approach for Internet governance. For example:

- India, Brazil, and South Africa (referred to as IBSA) proposed that "an appropriate body is urgently required in the U.N. system to coordinate and evolve coherent and integrated global public policies pertaining to the Internet." The IBSA proposed body would "integrate and oversee the bodies responsible for technical and operational functioning of the Internet, including global standards setting."[53]
- In order to implement the major aspects of the IBSA proposal, the government of India proposed (in the U.N. General Assembly) the establishment of a new institutional mechanism in the United Nations for global Internet-related policies, to be called the United Nations Committee for Internet-Related Policies (CIRP). CIRP would be comprised of 50 member states chosen on the basis of equitable geographical representation. The Internet Governance Forum (IGF) and four advisory stakeholder groups would provide input to CIRP, which would report directly to the General Assembly and present recommendations for consideration, adoption, and dissemination among all relevant intergovernmental bodies and international organizations.[54]
- Another group of nations, including China and the Russian Federation, proposed a voluntary "International Code of Conduct for Information Security," for further discussion in the U.N. General Assembly. The Code includes language that promotes the establishment of a multilateral, transparent, and democratic international management system to ensure an equitable distribution of resources, facilitate access for all, and ensure a stable and secure functioning of the Internet.[55]
- On January 13, 2015, the same group of nations released a revised International Code of Conduct for Information Security which states that

> all States must play the same role in, and carry equal responsibility for, international governance of the Internet, its security, continuity and stability of operation, and its development in a way which promotes the establishment of multilateral, transparent and democratic international Internet governance mechanisms which ensure an equitable distribution of resources, facilitate access for all and ensure the stable and secure functioning of the Internet.[56]

Thus, governments such as the United States and the European Union support ICANN's multistakeholder model, while at the same time advocating increased governmental influence within that model.[57] By contrast, other nations support an expanded role for an intergovernmental model of Internet governance. The debate has been summarized by NTIA as follows:

> By engaging all interested parties, multistakeholder processes encourage broader and more creative problem solving, which is essential when markets and technology are changing as rapidly as they are. They promote speedier, more flexible decision making than is common under traditional, top-down regulatory models which can too easily fall prey to rigid procedures, bureaucracy, and stalemate. But there is a challenge emerging to this model in parts of the world.... Some nations appear to prefer an Internet managed and controlled by nation-states. In December 2012, the U.S. will participate in the ITU's World Conference on International Telecommunications (WCIT). This treaty negotiation will conduct a review of the International Telecommunication Regulations (ITRs), the general principles which relate to traditional international voice telecommunication services. We expect that some states will attempt to rewrite the regulation in a manner that would exclude the contributions of multi-stakeholder organizations and instead provide for heavy-handed governmental control of the Internet, including provisions for cybersecurity and granular operational and technical requirements for private industry. We do not support any of these elements. It is critical that we work with the private sector on outreach to countries to promote the multi-stakeholder model as a credible alternative.[58]

World Conference on International Telecommunications (WCIT)

The World Conference on International Telecommunications (WCIT) was held in Dubai on December 3-14, 2012. Convened by the International Telecommunications Union (the ITU, an agency within the United Nations), the WCIT was a formal meeting of the world's national governments held in order to revise the International Telecommunications Regulations (ITRs). The ITRs, previously revised in 1988, serve as a global treaty outlining the principles which govern the way international telecommunications traffic is handled.

Because the existing 24-year-old ITRs predated the Internet, one of the key policy questions in the WCIT was how and to what extent the updated ITRs should address Internet traffic and Internet governance. The Administration and Congress took the position that the new ITRs should continue to address only traditional international telecommunications traffic, that a multistakeholder model of Internet governance (such as ICANN) should continue, and that the ITU should not take any action that could extend its jurisdiction or authority over the Internet.

As the WCIT approached, concerns heightened in the 112th Congress that the WCIT might potentially provide a forum leading to an increased level of intergovernmental control over the Internet. On May 31, 2012, the House Committee on Energy and Commerce, Subcommittee on Communications and Technology, held a hearing entitled, "International Proposals to Regulate the Internet."[59] To accompany the hearing, H.Con.Res. 127 was introduced by Representative Bono Mack expressing the sense of Congress regarding actions to preserve and advance the multistakeholder governance model. Specifically, H.Con.Res. 127 expressed the sense of Congress that the Administration "should continue working to implement the position of the United States on Internet governance that clearly articulates the consistent and unequivocal policy of the United States to promote a global Internet free from government control and preserve and advance the successful multistakeholder model that governs the Internet today." H.Con.Res. 127 was passed unanimously by the House (414-0) on August 2, 2012.

A similar resolution, S.Con.Res. 50, was introduced into the Senate by Senator Rubio on June 27, 2012, and referred to the Committee on Foreign Relations. The Senate resolution expressed the sense of Congress "that the Secretary of State, in consultation with the Secretary of

Commerce, should continue working to implement the position of the United States on Internet governance that clearly articulates the consistent and unequivocal policy of the United States to promote a global Internet free from government control and preserve and advance the successful multistakeholder model that governs the Internet today." S.Con.Res. 50 was passed by the Senate by unanimous consent on September 22, 2012. On December 5, 2012—shortly after the WCIT had begun in Dubai—the House unanimously passed S.Con.Res. 50 by a vote of 397-0.

During the WCIT, a revision to the ITRs was proposed and supported by Russia, China, Saudi Arabia, Algeria, and Sudan that sought to explicitly extend ITR jurisdiction over Internet traffic, infrastructure, and governance. Specifically, the proposal stated that "Member States shall have the sovereign right to establish and implement public policy, including international policy, on matters of Internet governance."[60] The proposal also included an article establishing the right of Member States to manage Internet numbering, naming, addressing, and identification resources.

The proposal was subsequently withdrawn. However, as an intended compromise, the ITU adopted a nonbinding resolution (Resolution 3, attached to the final ITR text) entitled, "To Foster an enabling environment for the greater growth of the Internet." Resolution 3 included language stating "all governments should have an equal role and responsibility for international Internet governance" and invited Member States to "elaborate on their respective positions on international Internet-related technical, development and public policy issues within the mandate of ITU at various ITU forums."[61]

Because of the inclusion of Resolution 3, along with other features of the final ITR text (such as new ITU articles related to spam and cybersecurity), the United States declined to sign the treaty. The leader of the U.S. delegation stated the following:

The Internet has given the world unimaginable economic and social benefits during these past 24 years—all without UN regulation. We candidly cannot support an ITU treaty that is inconsistent with a multi-stakeholder model of Internet governance. As the ITU has stated, this conference was never meant to focus on internet issues; however, today we are in a situation where we still have text and resolutions that cover issues on spam and also provisions on internet governance. These past two weeks, we have of course made good progress and shown a willingness to negotiate on a variety of telecommunications policy issues, such as roaming and settlement rates, but the United States continues to believe that internet policy must be multi-stakeholder driven. Internet

> policy should not be determined by member states but by citizens, communities, and broader society, and such consultation from the private sector and civil society is paramount. This has not happened here.[62]

As the WCIT approached, concerns heightened in the 112th Congress that the WCIT might potentially provide a forum leading to an increased level of intergovernmental control over the Internet. On May 31, 2012, the House Committee on Energy and Commerce, Subcommittee on Communications and Technology, held a hearing entitled, "International Proposals to Regulate the Internet."[59] To accompany the hearing, H.Con.Res. 127 was introduced by Representative Bono Mack expressing the sense of Congress regarding actions to preserve and advance the multistakeholder governance model. Specifically, H.Con.Res. 127 expressed the sense of Congress that the Administration "should continue working to implement the position of the United States on Internet governance that clearly articulates the consistent and unequivocal policy of the United States to promote a global Internet free from government control and preserve and advance the successful multistakeholder model that governs the Internet today." H.Con.Res. 127 was passed unanimously by the House (414-0) on August 2, 2012.

A similar resolution, S.Con.Res. 50, was introduced into the Senate by Senator Rubio on June 27, 2012, and referred to the Committee on Foreign Relations. The Senate resolution expressed the sense of Congress "that the Secretary of State, in consultation with the Secretary of Commerce, should continue working to implement the position of the United States on Internet governance that clearly articulates the consistent and unequivocal policy of the United States to promote a global Internet free from government control and preserve and advance the successful multistakeholder model that governs the Internet today." S.Con.Res. 50 was passed by the Senate by unanimous consent on September 22, 2012. On December 5, 2012—shortly after the WCIT had begun in Dubai—the House unanimously passed S.Con.Res. 50 by a vote of 397-0.

During the WCIT, a revision to the ITRs was proposed and supported by Russia, China, Saudi Arabia, Algeria, and Sudan that sought to explicitly extend ITR jurisdiction over Internet traffic, infrastructure, and governance. Specifically, the proposal stated that "Member States shall have the sovereign right to establish and implement public policy, including international policy, on matters of Internet governance."[60] The proposal also included an article establishing the right of Member States to manage Internet numbering, naming, addressing, and identification resources.

The proposal was subsequently withdrawn. However, as an intended compromise, the ITU adopted a nonbinding resolution (Resolution 3, attached to the final ITR text) entitled, "To Foster an enabling environment for the greater growth of the Internet." Resolution 3 included language stating "all governments should have an equal role and responsibility for international Internet governance" and invited Member States to "elaborate on their respective positions on international Internet-related technical, development and public policy issues within the mandate of ITU at various ITU forums."[61]

Because of the inclusion of Resolution 3, along with other features of the final ITR text (such as new ITU articles related to spam and cybersecurity), the United States declined to sign the treaty. The leader of the U.S. delegation stated the following:

> The Internet has given the world unimaginable economic and social benefits during these past 24 years—all without UN regulation. We candidly cannot support an ITU treaty that is inconsistent with a multi-stakeholder model of Internet governance. As the ITU has stated, this conference was never meant to focus on internet issues; however, today we are in a situation where we still have text and resolutions that cover issues on spam and also provisions on internet governance. These past two weeks, we have of course made good progress and shown a willingness to negotiate on a variety of telecommunications policy issues, such as roaming and settlement rates, but the United States continues to believe that internet policy must be multi-stakeholder driven. Internet policy should not be determined by member states but by citizens, communities, and broader society, and such consultation from the private sector and civil society is paramount. This has not happened here.[62]

Of the 144 eligible members of the ITU, 89 nations signed the treaty, while 55 either chose not to sign (such as the United States) or remain undecided.[63]

While the WCIT in Dubai is concluded, the international debate over Internet governance is expected to continue in future intergovernmental telecommunications meetings and conferences. The 113th Congress oversaw and supported the U.S. government's continuing efforts to resist international attempts to exert control over Internet governance. On February 5, 2013, the House Committee on Energy and Commerce, Subcommittee on Communications and Technology, held a hearing entitled "Fighting for Internet Freedom: Dubai and Beyond." The hearing was held jointly with the

House Committee on Foreign Affairs, Subcommittee on Terrorism, Nonproliferation, and Trade and the Subcommittee on Africa, Global Health, Global Human Rights, and International Organizations.

On April 16, 2013, H.R. 1580, a bill "To Affirm the Policy of the United States Regarding Internet Governance," was introduced by Representative Walden. Using language similar to the WCIT-related congressional resolutions passed by the 112th Congress (S.Con.Res. 50 and H.Con.Res. 127), H.R. 1580 stated that "It is the policy of the United States to preserve and advance the successful multistakeholder model that governs the Internet." On May 14, 2013, H.R. 1580 was passed unanimously (413-0) by the House of Representatives.

Montevideo Statement on the Future of Internet Cooperation

In October 2013, the President of ICANN and the leaders of other major organizations responsible for globally coordinating Internet technical infrastructure[64] met in Montevideo, Uruguay, and released a statement calling for strengthening the current mechanisms for global multistakeholder Internet cooperation. Their recommendations included the following:

- They reinforced the importance of globally coherent Internet operations, and warned against Internet fragmentation at a national level. They expressed strong concern over the undermining of the trust and confidence of Internet users globally due to recent revelations of pervasive monitoring and surveillance.
- They identified the need for ongoing effort to address Internet Governance challenges, and agreed to catalyze community-wide efforts towards the evolution of global multistakeholder Internet cooperation.
- They called for accelerating the globalization of ICANN and IANA functions, towards an environment in which all stakeholders, including all governments, participate on an equal footing.65

NETmundial

The day after the Montevideo Statement was released, the President of ICANN met with the President of Brazil, who announced plans to hold an international Internet governance summit in April 2014 that would include representatives from government, industry, civil society, and academia. NETmundial, which was described as a "global multistakeholder meeting on the future of Internet governance," was held on April 23-24, 2014, in Sao Paulo, Brazil.[66] The meeting was open to all interested stakeholders, and was intended to "focus on crafting Internet governance principles and proposing a roadmap for the further evolution of the Internet governance ecosystem."[67]

The outcome of NETmundial produced a nonbinding "NETmundial Multistakeholder Statement"[68] that set forth general Internet governance principles and identified issues to be discussed at future meetings on the future evolution of Internet governance. According to the U.S. government delegation at NETmundial, the meeting outcome reaffirmed the multistakeholder model of Internet governance, endorsed the transition of the U.S. government's stewardship role of IANA functions to the global multistakeholder community, emphasized the importance of strengthening and expanding upon the mandate of the Internet Governance Forum, and underscored the importance of human rights in the implementation of a free and open Internet.[69]

NETmundial Initiative

On August 28, 2014, the creation of a NETmundial Initiative for Internet Governance Cooperation and Development was announced by the World Economic Forum in partnership with ICANN and other governmental, industry, academic, and civil society stakeholders. While having no formal relationship with the April 2014 NETmundial summit held in Brazil, the purpose of the NETmundial Initiative is "to apply the NETmundial Principles to solve issues in concrete ways to enable an effective and distributed approach to Internet cooperation and governance."[70]

2014 Plenipotentiary Conference in Busan

The ITU's three-week Plenipotentiary Conference in Busan, Republic of Korea, concluded on November 7, 2014. The purpose of the conference, which meets every four years, is to set ITU general policies, adopt four-year strategic and financial plans, and elect ITU officials. Prior to the conference, the U.S. delegation (headed by the State Department) had concerns that some ITU members would attempt to expand ITU's role in Internet governance. In the view of the State Department, the conference concluded successfully, with "the member states decid[ing] not to expand the ITU's role in Internet governance or cybersecurity issues, accepting that many of those issues are outside of the mandate of the ITU."[71]

WSIS+10

On December 15-16, 2015, the United Nations General Assembly is holding a high-level meeting in New York to review the implementation of outcomes of the World Summit on the Information Society (WSIS). The meeting has been preceded by an intergovernmental process that takes into account inputs from all relevant WSIS stakeholders.[72] During this process, some nations have argued for an enhanced role for national governments in Internet governance and the internationalization of ICANN and the domain name system.[73]

Internet Governance and Terrorism

In the wake of the November 13, 2015, terrorist attack in Paris, and with ongoing concern over the use of the Internet by terrorist organizations, the question has arisen whether Internet governance mechanisms could be used to combat the use of the Internet by terrorist entities. Traditionally, nation-states can govern the use and content of the Internet within their national boundaries and many have the authority, pursuant to their respective national laws, to monitor, block, and/or shut down websites within their borders.[74] In some instances, these powers and actions have been controversial when, for example, antiterrorism concerns may be used to justify censorship or the suppression of free speech on the Internet.[75]

On an international level, governance of the Internet with respect to its content and use is problematic. As discussed earlier in this report, the Internet is decentralized and its functioning relies on the cooperation and participation by mostly private sector stakeholders around the world. As such, there is no international governance entity that currently has authority to remove global Internet content used to promote terrorism. While there have been proposals to establish some level of authority over the Internet by the United Nations, these proposals have originated, for the most part, from regimes such as China, Russia, and Iran, and have been consistently opposed by the United States and other Western nations who fear that increased United Nations authority over the Internet would ultimately support censorship and suppression of free speech.[76]

Could ICANN—a functioning model of nongovernmental multistakeholder Internet governance—be deployed to restrict or limit the use of the global Internet by terrorist groups? Currently, ICANN administers the technological infrastructure of the Internet (domain names, Internet protocol numbers and standards) and explicitly does not regulate Internet content. Any attempt to change ICANN policy towards regulating Internet content would likely be strongly opposed by most of the Internet stakeholders who administer and set policy for ICANN through a consensus process.

ISSUES FOR CONGRESS

Congress plays an important role overseeing NTIA's stewardship of the domain name system and ICANN. The House Committee on Energy and Commerce and the Senate Committee on Commerce, Science, and Transportation have held numerous oversight hearings exploring ICANN's performance in general, as well as specific DNS issues that arise (e.g., the proposed gTLD expansion). Additionally, other committees, such as the House and Senate Judiciary Committees, maintain an interest in the DNS as it affects Internet policy issues such as intellectual property, privacy, and cybercrime. Since 1997, congressional committees have held 39 hearings on the DNS and ICANN.[77]

The 114th Congress is likely to closely examine NTIA's March 14, 2014, proposed transitioning of its authority over ICANN and the DNS to a wholly multistakeholder-driven entity. Congress will likely consider whether the proposed transition is in the best interest of the United States and in the best interest of the Internet. As a transition plan is developed by ICANN and the Internet community, Congress will likely monitor and evaluate that plan, and seek assurances that a DNS free of U.S. government stewardship will remain stable, secure, resilient, and open. As part of its examination, Congress will likely continue assessing to what extent ongoing and future intergovernmental telecommunications conferences constitute an opportunity for some nations to increase intergovernmental control over the Internet, and how effectively NTIA and other government agencies (such as the State Department) are working to counteract that threat.

Finally, the ongoing debate over Internet governance will likely have a significant impact on how other aspects of the Internet may be governed in the future, especially in such areas as intellectual property, privacy, law enforcement, Internet free speech, and cybersecurity. Looking forward, the institutional nature of Internet governance could have far-reaching implications on important policy decisions that will likely shape the future evolution of the Internet.

APPENDIX. ICANN BASICS

ICANN is a not-for-profit public benefit corporation headquartered in Los Angeles, CA, and incorporated under the laws of the state of California. ICANN is organized under the California Nonprofit Public Benefit Law for charitable and public purposes, and as such, is subject to legal oversight by the California attorney general. ICANN has been granted tax-exempt status by the federal government and the state of California.[78]

ICANN's organizational structure consists of a Board of Directors (BOD) advised by a network of supporting organizations and advisory committees that represent various Internet constituencies and interests (see *Figure A-1*). Policies are developed and issues are researched by these subgroups, who in turn advise the Board of Directors, which is responsible for making all final policy and operational decisions. The Board of Directors consists of 16 international and geographically diverse members, composed of one president, eight members selected by a Nominating Committee, two selected by the Generic Names Supporting Organization, two selected by the Address Supporting Organization, two selected by the Country-Code Names Supporting Organization, and one selected by the At-Large Advisory Committee. Additionally, there are five nonvoting liaisons representing other advisory committees.

The explosive growth of the Internet and domain name registration, increasing responsibilities in managing and operating the DNS, and the rollout of the new gTLD program has led to marked growth of the ICANN budget, from revenues of about $6 million and a staff of 14 in 2000, to total support and revenue of $159 million and a headcount of 373 budgeted for 2015.[79] ICANN has been traditionally funded primarily through fees paid to ICANN by registrars and registry operators. Registrars are companies (e.g., GoDaddy, Google, Network Solutions) with which consumers register domain names.[80] Registry operators are companies and organizations that operate and administer the master database of all domain names registered in each top level domain (for example VeriSign, Inc. operates .com and .net, Public Interest Registry operates .org, and Neustar, Inc. operates .biz).[81]

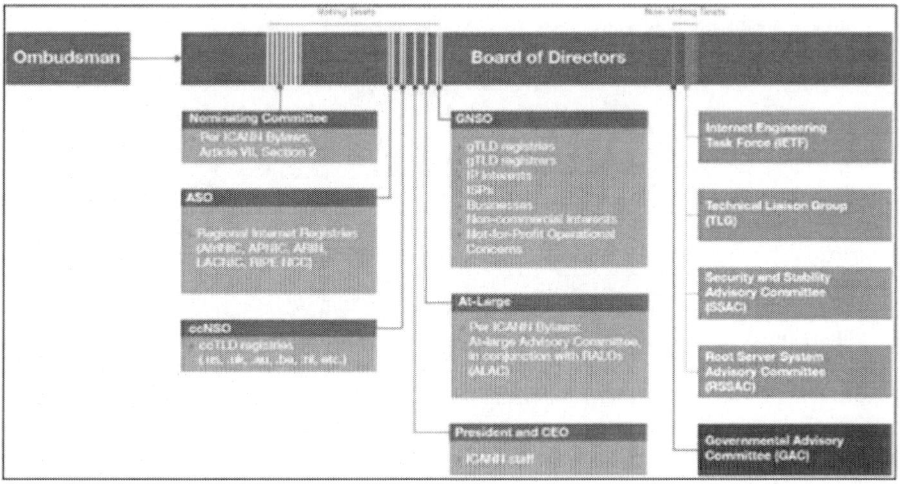

Source: ICANN; http://www.icann.org/en/groups/chart.

Figure A-1. Organizational Structure of ICANN.

End Notes

[1] Tunis Agenda for the Information Society, November 18, 2005, WSIS-05/TUNIS/DOC6 (Rev.1)-E, p. 6, available at http://www.itu.int/wsis/docs2/tunis/off/6rev1.pdf.

[2] The IGP describes itself as "an alliance of academics that puts expertise into practical action in the fields of global governance, Internet policy, and information and communication technology." See http://www.internetgovernance.org.

[3] Milton Mueller, John Mathiason, and Hans Klein, "The Internet and Global Governance: Principles and Norms for a New Regime," Global Governance, vol. 13 (2007), p. 245.

[4] For more information on the Affirmation of Commitments, including the precursor agreements between DOC and ICANN such as the Joint Project Agreement and the Memorandum of Understanding, see CRS Report 97-868, Internet Domain Names: Background and Policy Issues, by Lennard G. Kruger.

[5] Affirmation of Commitments by the U.S. Department of Commerce and the Internet Corporation for Assigned Names and Numbers, September 30, 2009, available at http://www.ntia.doc.gov/ntiahome/domainname/Affirmation_of_Commitments_2009.pdf.

[6] WHOIS is a publicly available online database that provides information on domain name registrants. WHOIS is used to identify domain name holders. WHOIS policy is controversial because it encompasses two competing considerations: protecting the privacy of domain name holders versus enabling law enforcement and trademark holders to identify owners of domain names and websites engaging in criminal activities or infringing on intellectual property.

[7] The ATRT final report is available at http://www.icann.org/en/reviews/affirmation/atrt-final-recommendations31dec10-en.pdf.

[8] NTIA, Press Release, "NTIA Commends ICANN Board on Adopting the Recommendations of the Accountability and Transparency Review Team," June 24, 2011, available at http://www.ntia.doc.gov/press/2011/NTIA_Statement_06242011.html.

[9] Internet Assigned Numbers Authority.

[10] According to the National Research Council, "The root zone file defines the DNS. For all practical purposes, a top level domain (and, therefore, all of its lower-level domains) is in the DNS if and only if it is listed in the root zone file. Therefore, presence in the root determines which DNS domains are available on the Internet." See National Research Council, Committee on Internet Navigation and the Domain Name System, Technical Alternatives and Policy Implications, Signposts on Cyberspace: The Domain Name System and Internet Navigation, National Academy Press, Washington, DC, 2005, p. 97.

[11] The June 30, 2005, "U.S. Principles on the Internet's Domain Name and Addressing System" stated the intention to "preserve the security and stability" of the DNS, and asserted that "the United States is committed to taking no action that would have the potential to adversely impact the effective and efficient operation of the DNS and will therefore maintain its historic role in authorizing changes or modifications to the authoritative root zone file." See http://www.ntia.doc.gov/ntiahome/domainname/USDNSprinciples_06302005.pdf.

[12] For a full discussion of this issue, see CRS Report R44022, The Future of Internet Governance: Should the United States Relinquish Its Authority over ICANN?, by Lennard G. Kruger.

[13] NTIA, Press Release, "NTIA Announced Intent to Transition Key Internet Domain Name Functions," March 14, 2014, available at http://www.ntia.doc.gov/press-release/2014/ntia-announces-intent-transition-key-internet-domainname-functions.

[14] ICANN, "Montevideo Statement on the Future of Internet Cooperation," October 7, 2013, available at https://www.icann.org/en/news/announcements/announcement-07oct13-en.htm.

[15] ICANN, "Endorsements of the IANA Globalization Process," March 18, 2014, available at https://www.icann.org/en/about/agreements/iana/globalization-endorsements-18mar14-en.pdf.

[16] The Commerce Department's June 10, 1998 Statement of Policy stated that the U.S. government "is committed to a transition that will allow the private sector to take leadership for DNS management." Available at http://www.ntia.doc.gov/legacy/ntiahome/domainname/6_5_98dns.htm.

[17] NTIA, Press Release, "NTIA Announced Intent to Transition Key Internet Domain Name Functions," March 14, 2014.

[18] See for example: Atkinson, Rob, "U.S. Giving Up Its Internet 'Bodyguard' Role," March 17, 2014, available at http://www.ideaslaboratory.com/2014/03/17/u-s-giving-up-its-internet-bodyguard-role/; and Nagesh, Gauthem, Wall Street Journal, "U.S. Plan for Web Faces Credibility Issue," March 18, 2014.

[19] Hearing before the House Energy and Commerce Committee, Subcommittee on Communications and Technology, "Ensuring the Security, Stability, Resilience, and Freedom of the Global Internet," April 2, 2014, available at http://energycommerce.house.gov/hearing/ensuring-security-stability-resilience-and-freedom-global-internet.

[20] See http://energycommerce.house.gov/sites/republicans.energycommerce.house.gov/files/letters/20140605GAO.pdf.

[21] Testimony available at http://www.commerce.senate.gov/public/index.cfm?p=Hearings.

[22] Testimony available at http://energycommerce.house.gov/hearing/stakeholder-perspectives-iana-transition.

[23] Testimony available at http://judiciary.house.gov/index.cfm/hearings?ID=7E5AF16E-B1F8-45B8-803B9E389A9B745E.

[24] Testimony available at http://energycommerce.house.gov/hearing/internet-governance-progress-after-icann-53.

[25] Available at http://www.cruz.senate.gov/files/documents/Letters/
20150922%20Grassley%20Cruz%20Goodlatte%20Issa%20GAO%20Request%20ICANN.pdf.

[26] Available at https://regmedia.co.uk/2015/10/16/thune-schatz-icann-oct15.pdf.

[27] Working Group on Internet Governance, Report from the Working Group on Internet Governance, World Summit on the Information Society, Document WSIS-II/PC-3/DOC/5-E, August 3, 2005, available at http://www.itu.int/wsis/docs2/pc3/html/off5/index.html.

[28] In the 109th Congress, H.Con.Res. 268 was passed unanimously by the House on November 16, 2005. S.Res. 323 was passed in the Senate by Unanimous Consent on November 18, 2005.

[29] See McCarthy, Kieren, .nxt, "Global Internet Governance Fight Looms," September 22, 2011, available at http://news.dot-nxt.com/2011/09/22/internet-governance-fight-looms.

[30] ICANN, Adopted Board Resolutions, Cartegena, December 10, 2010, available at http://www.icann.org/en/minutes/resolutions-10dec10-en.htm#4.

[31] Letter from Chair, Governmental Advisory Committee to ICANN Chairman of the Board, March 16, 2011, available at https://gacweb.icann.org/download/attachments/1540116/20110316+GAC+Advice+on+.xxx.pdf?version=2& modificationDate=1312469527000.

[32] Letter from ICANN to Chair of GAC, February 10, 2011, available at http://icann.org/en/correspondence/jeffrey-toto-dryden-10feb11-en.pdf.

[33] ICANN must receive formal approval from NTIA for any additions of new gTLDs to the DNS. See Kevin Murphy, "US upset with ICANN over .xxx," Domain Incite, March 20, 2011, available at http://domainincite.com/us-upsetwith-icann-over-xxx/. India and Saudi Arabia have stated their intention to block the .xxx domain. See "xxx addresses open for business," The Times of India, April 19, 2011, available at http://articles.timesofindia.indiatimes.com/2011-04-19/computing/29446429_1_icann-suffix-websites.

[34] Kevin Murphy, "Europe asked US to delay .xxx," Domain Incite, May 5, 2011, available at http://domainincite.com/europe-did-ask-the-us-to-delay-xxx/.

[35] Letter from Lawrence Strickling to Neelie Kroes, "Strickling letter to Kroes re: dot-xxx," .nxt, April 20, 2011, available at http://news.dot-nxt.com/2011/04/20/strickling-letter-kroes-xxx.

[36] Ibid.

[37] The Association of National Advertisers (ANA) has been a leading voice against ICANN's current rollout of the new gTLD program. See ANA web page, "Say No to ICANN: Generic Top Level Domain Developments," available at http://www.ana.net/content/show/id/icann.

[38] See "Rockefeller Says Internet Domain Expansion Will Hurt Consumers, Businesses, and Non-Profits—Urges Delay," Press Release, Senate Committee on Commerce, Science and Transportation, December 28, 2011, available at http://commerce.senate.gov/public/index.cfm?p=PressReleases.

[39] Letter from Senator Amy Klobuchar and Senator Kelly Ayotte to ICANN, December 22, 2011, available at http://www.icann.org/en/correspondence/klobuchar-ayotte-to-beckstrom-crocker-22dec11-en.pdf.

[40] House Committee on Energy and Commerce, "Committee Urges ICANN to Delay Expansion of Generic Top-Level Domain Program," Press Release, December 21, 2011, available at http://energycommerce.house.gov/news/PRArticle.aspx?NewsID=9176.

[41] Ibid.

[42] Letter from Representative Goodlatte and Representative Berman to the Secretary of Commerce, December 16, 2011, available at http://www.icann.org/en/correspondence/goodlatte-berman-to-bryson-16dec11-en.pdf.

[43] Letter from FTC to ICANN, December 16, 2011, available at http://www.ftc.gov/os/closings/publicltrs/111216letterto-icann.pdf.

[44] Letter from the Chairmen and Ranking Members of the Senate and House Judiciary Committees to Rod Beckstrom, CEO, ICANN, December 27, 2011, available at http://www.icann.org/en/correspondence/leahy-to-beckstrom-27dec11- en.pdf.

[45] Testimony of Kurt Pritz, Senior Vice President, ICANN, before the House Committee on Energy and Commerce, Subcommittee on Communications and Technology, December 14, 2011, available at http://republicans.energycommerce.house.gov/Media/file/Hearings/Telecom/121411/Pritz.pdf. The gTLD expansion is also strongly supported by many in the Internet and domain name industry, see letter to Senator Rockefeller and Senator Hutchison at http://news.dot-nxt.com/sites/news.dot-nxt.com/files/gtld-industry-to-congress-gtlds-8dec11.pdf.

[46] Testimony of Fiona M. Alexander, Associate Administrator, NTIA, before the House Committee on Energy and Commerce, Subcommittee on Communications and Technology, December 14, 2011, available at http://www.ntia.doc.gov/speechtestimony/2011/testimony-associate-administrator-alexander-icann-s-top-level-domain name-progr.

[47] Ibid.

[48] Letter from Lawrence Strickling, Assistant Secretary for Communications and Information, U.S. Department of Commerce, to ICANN, January 3, 2012, available at http://www.ntia.doc.gov/other-publication/2012/ntia-letterregarding-gtld-program.

[49] Ibid.

[50] Ibid., Module 3, p. 3-3.

[51] Organisation for Economic Co-operation and Development, OECD High Level Meeting, The Internet Economy: Generating Innovation and Growth, Communique on Principles for Internet Policy-Making, June 28-29, 2011, p. 4, available at http://www.oecd.org/dataoecd/33/12/48387430.pdf.

[52] G8 Declaration, Renewed Commitment for Freedom and Democracy, G8 Summit of Deauville, May 26-27, 2011, available at http://www.g20-g8.com/g8-g20/g8/english/live/news/renewed-commitment-for-freedom-anddemocracy.1314.html.

[53] IBSA Multistakeholder meeting on Global Internet Governance, Recommendations, September 1-2, 2011 at Rio de Janeiro, Brazil, available at http://www.culturalivre.org.br/artigos/IBSA_recommendations_Internet_Governance.pdf.

[54] The CIRP proposal is available at http://igfwatch.org/discussion-board/indias-proposal-for-a-un-committee-forinternet-related-policies-cirp.

[55] United Nations General Assembly, Sixty-sixth session, Item 93 of the provisional agenda, Developments in the field of information and telecommunications in the context of international security, "Letter dated 12 September 2011 from the Permanent Representatives of China, the Russian Federation, Tajikistan, and Uzbekistan to the United Nations addressed to the Secretary-General," September 14, 2011, A/66/359, available at http://blog.internetgovernance.org/pdf/UN-infosec-code.pdf.

[56] United Nations General Assembly, "Letter Dated 9 January 2015 from the Permanent Representatives of China, Kazakhstan, Kyrgyzstan, the Russian Federation, Tajikistan, and Uzbekistan to the United Nations Addressed to the Secretary General," January 13, 2015, p. 5, available at http://regmedia.co.uk/2015/02/04/un-internet-security13jan15.pdf.

[57] The European Commission has been a particularly strong voice in favor of significantly increasing GAC influence on the ICANN policy process. See Kieren McCarthy, "European Commission calls for greater government control over Internet," .nxt, August 31, 2011, available at http://news.dot-nxt.com/2011/08/31/ec-greater-government-control.

[58] Remarks by Lawrence Strickling, Assistant Secretary of Commerce for Communications and Information, National Telecommunications and Information Administration, Department of Commerce, before the PLI/FCBA Telecommunications Policy and Regulation Institute, Washington, DC, December 8, 2011, available at http://www.ntia.doc.gov/speeches timony/2011/remarks-assistant-secretary-strickling-prac tising-law-institutes-29thannual-te.

[59] Available at http://energycommerce.house.gov/hearings/hearingdetail.aspx?NewsID=9543.

[60] See Article 3A, "Proposals for the Work of the Conference," available at http://files. wcitleaks.org/public/Merged%20UAE%2008 1212.pdf.

[61] International Telecommunications Union, Final Acts, World Conference on International Telecommunications, Dubai, 2012, Resolution 3, p. 20, available at http://www.itu.int/ en/wcit-12/Documents/final-acts-wcit-12.pdf.

[62] Statement delivered by Ambassador Terry Kramer from the floor of the WCIT, December 13, 2012. U.S. Department of State, Press Release, "U.S. Intervention at the World Conference on International Telecommunications," December 13, 2012, available at http://www. state.gov/r/pa/prs/ps/2012/12/202037.htm.

[63] The official ITU list of signatories and non-signatories is at http://www.itu.int/osg/wcit-12/highlights/ signatories.html.

[64] The Internet Society, World Wide Web Consortium, Internet Engineering Task Force, Internet Architecture Board, and all five of the regional Internet address registries.

[65] Full statement is available at http://www.icann.org/en/news/announcements/announcement-07oct13-en.htm.

[66] Further information on NETmundial is available at http://netmundial.br/.

[67] Ibid.

[68] Available at http://netmundial.br/wp-content/uploads/2014/04/NETmundial-Multistakeholder-Document.pdf.

[69] United States Diplomatic Mission to Brazil, "Official Statement by the USG Delegation to NETmundial," April 25, 2014, available at http://brazil.usembassy.gov/statementusgdele tationnetmundial.html.

[70] World Economic Forum, NETmundial Initiative, available at http://www3.weforum.org/docs/ WEF_1NetmundialInitiativeBrief.pdf.

[71] U.S. Department of State, Media Note, "Outcomes from the International Telecommunication Union 2014 Plenipotentiary Conference in Busan, Republic of Korea," available at http://www.state.gov/r/pa/prs/ps/2014/11/233914.htm.

[72] Information on WSIS+10 is available at http://unpan3.un.org/wsis10/GA-High-Level-Meeting.

[73] See for example comments submitted to the U.N. General Assembly by China (http://workspace.unpan.org/sites/Internet/Documents/UNPAN95318.pdf) and Russia (http://workspace.unpan.org/sites/Internet/Documents/UNPAN95301.pdf).

[74] See for example, Conway, Maura, "Terrorism and Internet Governance: Core Issues," Disarmament Forum, 2007, pp. 23-34, available at http://www.peacepalacelibrary.nl/ ebooks/files/UNIDIR_pdf-art2644.pdf.

[75] See CRS Report R41837, Promoting Global Internet Freedom: Policy and Technology, by Patricia Moloney Figliola.

[76] For example, see the previous section on the 2012 World Conference International Telecommunications (WCIT) in this report.

[77] For a complete list, see the Appendix in CRS Report 97-868, Internet Domain Names: Background and Policy Issues, by Lennard G. Kruger.

[78] ICANN, 2008 Annual Report, December 31, 2008, p. 24, available at http://www.icann.org/en/annualreport/annualreport-2008-en.pdf.

[79] ICANN, FY15 Adopted Operating Plan and Budget, pp. 6, 10, available at https://www.icann.org/en/system/files/files/adopted-opplan-budget-fy15-01dec14-en.pdf.

[80] A list of ICANN-accredited registrars is available at http://www.icann.org/en/registries/agreements.htm.

[81] A list of current agreements between ICANN and registry operators is available at http://www.icann.org/en/registries/agreements.htm.

In: Internet Governance
Editor: Ernestine Saunders
ISBN: 978-1-63484-920-3

Chapter 2

THE FUTURE OF INTERNET GOVERNANCE: SHOULD THE UNITED STATES RELINQUISH ITS AUTHORITY OVER ICANN?*

Lennard G. Kruger

SUMMARY

Currently, the U.S. government retains limited authority over the Internet's domain name system, primarily through the Internet Assigned Numbers Authority (IANA) functions contract between the National Telecommunications and Information Administration (NTIA) and the Internet Corporation for Assigned Names and Numbers (ICANN). By virtue of the IANA functions contract, the NTIA exerts a legacy authority and stewardship over ICANN, and arguably has more influence over ICANN and the domain name system (DNS) than other national governments.

On March 14, 2014, NTIA announced the intention to transition its stewardship role and procedural authority over key Internet domain name functions to the global Internet multistakeholder community. To accomplish this transition, NTIA has asked ICANN to convene interested global Internet stakeholders to develop a transition proposal. NTIA has stated that it will not accept any transition proposal that would replace the

* This is an edited, reformatted and augmented version of a Congressional Research Service publication R44022, prepared for Members and Committees of Congress, dated November 3, 2015.

NTIA role with a government-led or an intergovernmental organization solution.

Internet stakeholders are engaged in a process to develop a transition proposal. While the IANA functions contract was due to expire on September 30, 2015, NTIA has the flexibility to extend the contract for any period through September 2019. NTIA expects that it will receive a final transition proposal in January 2016 with additional time necessary for review, testing, and implementation. On August 17, 2015, NTIA announced that the IANA contract will be extended for one year until September 30, 2016.

Concerns have risen in Congress over the proposed transition. Critics worry that relinquishing U.S. authority over Internet domain names may offer opportunities for either hostile foreign governments or intergovernmental organizations, such as the United Nations, to gain undue influence over the Internet. On the other hand, supporters argue that this transition completes the necessary evolution of Internet domain name governance towards the private sector, and will ultimately support and strengthen the multistakeholder model of Internet governance.

Legislation has been introduced in the 113th and 114th Congresses which would prevent, delay, or impose conditions or additional scrutiny on the transition. In the 114th Congress, H.R. 805/S. 1551 (the DOTCOM Act of 2015) would prohibit NTIA from relinquishing its authority until 30 legislative days after NTIA submits a report to Congress in which it certifies that the transition proposal meets certain criteria. On June 23, 2015, H.R. 805 was passed by the House. H.R. 2578 (FY2016 Commerce, Justice, Science (CJS) Appropriations Act), as passed by the House, directs that NTIA may not use any FY2016 appropriated funds to relinquish its responsibility with respect to Internet domain name system functions.

The proposed transition could have a significant impact on the future of Internet governance. National governments are recognizing an increasing stake in ICANN and DNS policy decisions, especially in cases where Internet DNS policy intersects with national laws and interests related to issues such as intellectual property, cybersecurity, privacy, and Internet freedom. How ICANN and the Internet domain name system are ultimately governed may set an important precedent in future policy debates—both domestically and internationally—over how the Internet should be governed, and what role governments and intergovernmental organizations should play.

BACKGROUND: THE DOMAIN NAME SYSTEM AND THE ROLE OF THE U.S. GOVERNMENT

The Internet is often described as a “network of networks” because it is not a single physical entity, but hundreds of thousands of interconnected networks linking hundreds of millions of computers around the world. As such, the Internet is international, decentralized, and comprised of networks and infrastructure largely owned and operated by private sector entities.[1]

Computers connected to the Internet are identified by a unique Internet Protocol (IP) number that designates their specific location, thereby making it possible to send and receive messages and to access information from computers anywhere on the Internet. Domain names were created to provide users with a simple location name, rather than requiring them to use a long list of numbers. The domain name system (DNS) is the distributed set of databases residing in computers around the world that contain the address numbers, mapped to corresponding domain names. Those computers, called root servers, must be coordinated to ensure connectivity across the Internet.

The U.S. government has no statutory authority over the DNS. However, because the Internet evolved from a network infrastructure created by the Department of Defense, the U.S. government originally owned and operated (primarily through private contractors) many of the key components of the network architecture that enabled the domain name system to function.[2] In 1998, with the Internet expanding beyond the academic and governmental spheres, the U.S. government transitioned the management of the DNS to a newly created not-for-profit international organization based in California called the Internet Corporation for Assigned Names and Numbers (ICANN).[3] ICANN employed (and continues to employ) a multistakeholder system of governance whereby policy decisions are made by a Board of Directors with input from the various stakeholder groups that comprise the Internet and the domain name system. These stakeholders include owners and operators of servers and networks around the world, domain name registrars and registries, regional IP address allocation organizations, standards organizations, Internet service providers, local and national governments, noncommercial stakeholders, business users, intellectual property interests, and others.

After the 1998 transition, the U.S. government, through the Department of Commerce’s National Telecommunications and Information Administration or NTIA, retained a degree of authority over ICANN’s management of the DNS and other unique Internet identifiers such as Internet address numbers and protocols. With respect to ICANN, the U.S. government first exercised its legacy authority through a Memorandum of Understanding (1998-2006), followed by a Joint Project Agreement (2006-2009). Currently, NTIA and ICANN are joint participants in an Affirmation of Commitments (AoC) agreement, in which both parties agree to scrutiny and evaluation by review boards. The AoC is voluntary, and either ICANN or NTIA can withdraw from the agreement at any time.[4]

Concurrently, a separate contract between the ICANN and NTIA—specifically referred to as the "IANA[5] functions contract"—authorizes ICANN to manage the technical underpinnings of the domain name system (DNS). The IANA functions can be broadly grouped into three categories:

1. Number resources—the coordination and allocation of the global pool of IP numbers;
2. Protocol Assignments—the management of IP numbering systems in conjunction with Internet standards bodies; and
3. Domain names—management of the DNS authoritative root zone file.[6]

Additionally, and intertwined with the IANA functions contract, a cooperative agreement between NTIA and VeriSign (the company that operates the .com and .net registries) authorizes VeriSign to manage and maintain the official root zone file that is contained in the Internet's root servers[7] which underlie the functioning of the DNS.[8]

The IANA functions contract gives the U.S. government, through NTIA, the authority to approve various technical functions such as modifying the root zone file (which would include, for example, adding additional generic top level domains (gTLDs) to the root zone). In this narrow sense, NTIA's role is strictly clerical and administrative.[9] Policymaking—such as decisions to make changes in the root zone file—are made by ICANN through its internal policy development process. Although it has the authority to do so under the IANA functions contract, NTIA has never refused to approve any IANA related actions as directed by ICANN.

However, the IANA functions contract, while primarily administrative in nature, carries broader significance because it has conferred upon the U.S. government a "stewardship" role over ICANN and the domain name system. This stewardship role does not mean that the NTIA controls ICANN or has the authority to approve or disapprove ICANN policy decisions. Rather, the U.S. government's authority over the IANA functions has been viewed by the

Internet community as a "backstop" that serves to reassure Internet users that the U.S. government is prepared and positioned to constitute a check on ICANN under extreme circumstances (such as, for example, fiscal insolvency, failure to meet operational obligations, or capture or undue influence by a single stakeholder or by outside interests).

Meanwhile, the U.S. government continues to participate in the ICANN policy development process through membership in the Governmental Advisory Committee (GAC), which provides advice to ICANN on issues of public policy, especially where there may be an interaction between ICANN's activities or policies and national laws or international agreements.[10] However, while all governments have access to membership in the GAC, the U.S. government arguably has had more influence over ICANN and the DNS than other governments by virtue of the IANA functions contract with ICANN.

NTIA Intent to Transition Stewardship of the DNS

On March 14, 2014, NTIA announced its intention to transition its stewardship role and procedural authority over key domain name functions to the global Internet multistakeholder community.[11] NTIA's stated intention was that it would let its IANA functions contract with ICANN expire on September 30, 2015, if a satisfactory transition could be achieved. With NTIA having the option of extending the contract for up to two two-year periods through September 30, 2019, NTIA announced on August 17, 2015, that it will extend the IANA functions contract through September 30, 2016.

As a first step, NTIA asked ICANN to convene interested global Internet stakeholders to develop a proposal to achieve the transition. Specifically, NTIA expects ICANN to work collaboratively with parties directly affected by the IANA contract, including the Internet Engineering Task Force (IETF), the Internet Architecture Board (IAB), the Internet Society (ISOC), the Regional Internet Registries (RIRs), top level domain name operators, Verisign, and other interested global stakeholders. In October 2013, many of these groups—specifically, the Internet technical organizations responsible for coordination of the Internet infrastructure—had called for "accelerating the globalization of ICANN and IANA functions, towards an environment in which all stakeholders, including all governments, participate on an equal footing."[12]

NTIA has stated that it will not accept any transition proposal that would replace the NTIA role with a government-led or an intergovernmental organization solution. In addition, NTIA told ICANN that the transition proposal must have broad community support and address the following four principles:

- support and enhance the multistakeholder model;
- maintain the security, stability, and resilience of the Internet DNS;
- meet the needs and expectation of the global customers and partners of the IANA services; and
- maintain the openness of the Internet.

MULTISTAKEHOLDER PROCESS TO DEVELOP A TRANSITION PROPOSAL

ICANN has convened a process through which the multistakeholder community will attempt to come to consensus on a transition proposal. The process is divided into two separate but related parallel processes: (1) IANA Stewardship Transition and (2) Enhancing ICANN Accountability. *Figure 1* shows a schematic diagram of the two interlinked processes. NTIA has stated that it views these two processes as "directly linked" and that "both issues must be addressed before any transition takes place."[13] The ICANN Board is expecting to receive both proposals at "roughly the same time" and will "forward them promptly and without modification to NTIA."[14]

IANA Stewardship Transition

Based on feedback received from the Internet community at its March 2014 meeting in Singapore, ICANN put out for public input and comment a draft proposal of *Principles, Mechanisms and Process to Develop a Proposal to Transition NTIA's Stewardship of the IANA Functions*.[15] Under the draft proposal, a steering group was formed "to steward the process in an open, transparent, inclusive, and accountable manner."[16] The steering group was composed of representatives of each ICANN constituency and of parties directly affected by the transition of IANA functions (for example, Internet standards groups and Internet number resource organizations).

On June 6, 2014, after receiving public comments on the steering group draft proposal, ICANN announced the formation of a Coordination Group which is responsible for preparing a transition proposal.[17] The IANA Stewardship Transition Coordination Group (ICG) is composed of 30 individuals representing 13 Internet stakeholder communities.[18] On August 27, 2014, the ICG released its charter, which stated that its mission is "to coordinate the development of a proposal among the communities affected by the IANA functions."[19]

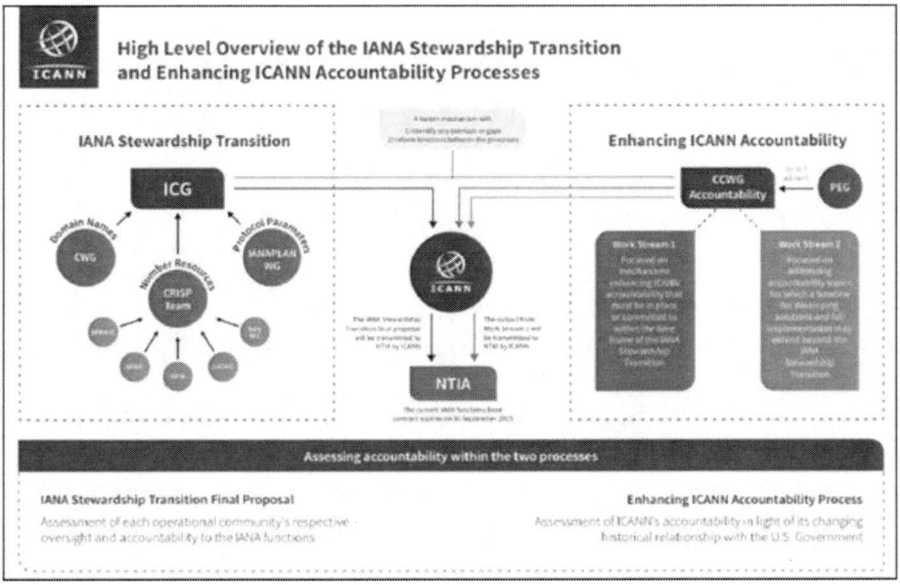

Source: ICANN.

Notes: ICG = IANA Stewardship Transition Coordination Group; CRISP = Consolidated Regional Internet Registries (RIR) IANA Stewardship Proposal Team; CWG = Cross Community Working Group on Naming Related Functions; CCWG = Accountability Cross Community Working Group; PEG = Public Experts Group.

Figure 1. Schematic of Process to Develop IANA Transition Proposal.

The ICG requested a proposal for each of the three primary IANA functions (domain name-related functions, numbering, and protocol parameters) to be developed by the three operational communities associated with each of those primary functions. Upon receipt of the three proposals, the ICG worked to develop a single consolidated proposal. The three proposals and break out as follows:

- Number Resources—developed by the five Regional Internet Registries (RIR) via the Consolidated RIR IANA Stewardship Proposal Team (CRISP Team).
- Protocol Parameters—developed by the Internet Engineering Task Force (IETF) through the IANAPLAN Working Group (IANAPLAN WG).
- Domain Names—developed by the Cross Community Working Group to Develop an IANA Stewardship Transition Proposal on Naming Related Functions (CWG-Stewardship).

While the Number Resources and the Protocol Parameter proposals were completed in January 2015, consensus on a domain name function proposal proved more difficult to reach, with the CWG-Stewardship group unable to meet an initial January 2015 deadline. This is perhaps due to the fact that both numbering and protocols are currently operated by external groups which already perform these activities under contract with ICANN. The domain name IANA function is performed by ICANN itself (under contract to NTIA), and the question of how to transition away from the NTIA contract with respect to the domain naming function is inherently more complex and controversial.

The CWG-Stewardship group is composed of 19 members appointed by chartering organizations and 115 participants who contributed to mailing list conversations and meetings. The key question the group has grappled with is whether a new organization or entity should be created to oversee the IANA functions contract (an external model), or whether ICANN itself—subject to enhanced accountability measures—should be given authority over the IANA function (an internal model).

Proposal

On July 31, 2015, the ICG released its IANA Transition Stewardship Proposal for public comment. The proposal combines the three proposals developed for Numbers Resources, Protocol Parameters, and Domain Names:

- Numbers Resources—the numbers community proposed that ICANN continue to serve as the IANA Functions Operator and perform those services under a contract with the five Regional Internet Registries (RIRs). The numbers community also proposed a contractual Service Level Agreement between the RIRs and the IANA Numbering Service Operator and a Review Committee comprising community representatives from each region to advise the RIRs on the IANA functions operator's performance and adherence to identified service levels.

- Protocol Parameters—the protocol parameters community proposed to continue to rely on the current system of agreements, policies and oversight mechanisms created by the IETF, ICANN, and IAB for the provisions of the protocols parameters-related IANA functions.
- Domain Names—the domain names community proposed to form a new, separate legal entity, Post-Transition IANA (PTI), as an affiliate (subsidiary) of ICANN that would become the IANA functions operator in contract with ICANN. This proposal integrates elements of both the internal and external models. ICANN would assume the role currently fulfilled by NTIA (overseeing the IANA function), while PTI would assume the role currently played by ICANN (the IANA functions operator).The legal jurisdiction in which ICANN resides (California) is to remain unchanged. The proposal includes the creation of a Customer Standing Committee (CSC) responsible for monitoring the operator's performance according to the contractual requirements and service level expectations. The proposal establishes a multistakeholder IANA Function Review process (IFR) to conduct review of PTI.

On October 29, 2015, the ICG announced that it had incorporated public comments into its final transition proposal[20] and had completed its work. The domain names portion of the proposal is conditioned on the completion of the ICANN Accountability proposal. The numbers and protocol parameters portions of the proposal are complete and ready for implementation.[21]

The CWG-Stewardship group is composed of 19 members appointed by chartering organizations and 115 participants who contributed to mailing list conversations and meetings. The key question the group has grappled with is whether a new organization or entity should be created to oversee the IANA functions contract (an external model), or whether ICANN itself—subject to enhanced accountability measures—should be given authority over the IANA function (an internal model).

Proposal

On July 31, 2015, the ICG released its IANA Transition Stewardship Proposal for public comment. The proposal combines the three proposals developed for Numbers Resources, Protocol Parameters, and Domain Names:

- Numbers Resources—the numbers community proposed that ICANN continue to serve as the IANA Functions Operator and perform those services under a contract with the five Regional Internet Registries (RIRs). The numbers community also proposed a contractual Service Level Agreement between the RIRs and the IANA Numbering Service Operator and a Review Committee comprising community representatives from each region to advise the RIRs on the IANA functions operator's performance and adherence to identified service levels.
- Protocol Parameters—the protocol parameters community proposed to continue to rely on the current system of agreements, policies and oversight mechanisms created by the IETF, ICANN, and IAB for the provisions of the protocols parameters-related IANA functions.
- Domain Names—the domain names community proposed to form a new, separate legal entity, Post-Transition IANA (PTI), as an affiliate (subsidiary) of ICANN that would become the IANA functions operator in contract with ICANN. This proposal integrates elements of both the internal and external models. ICANN would assume the role currently fulfilled by NTIA (overseeing the IANA function), while PTI would assume the role currently played by ICANN (the IANA functions operator).The legal jurisdiction in which ICANN resides (California) is to remain unchanged. The proposal includes the creation of a Customer Standing Committee (CSC) responsible for monitoring the operator's performance according to the contractual requirements and service level expectations. The proposal establishes a multistakeholder IANA Function Review process (IFR) to conduct review of PTI.

On October 29, 2015, the ICG announced that it had incorporated public comments into its final transition proposal[20] and had completed its work. The domain names portion of the proposal is conditioned on the completion of the ICANN Accountability proposal. The numbers and protocol parameters portions of the proposal are complete and ready for implementation.[21]

Enhancing ICANN Accountability

In parallel with the IANA stewardship transition process, ICANN initiated a separate but related process on how to enhance ICANN's accountability. The purpose of this process is to ensure that ICANN will remain accountable to Internet stakeholders if and when ICANN is no longer subject to the IANA contract with the U.S. government. Specifically, the process is to examine how ICANN's broader accountability mechanisms should be strengthened to address the potential absence of its historical contractual relationship with the DOC, including looking at strengthening existing accountability mechanisms (e.g., the ICANN bylaws and the Affirmation of Commitments).

To implement the accountability process, ICANN formed a Cross Community Working Group (CCWG) to develop proposals to enhance ICANN's accountability towards all stakeholders.[22] The CCWG is pursuing two interrelated Work Streams. Work Stream 1 focuses on mechanisms enhancing ICANN accountability that must be in place or committed to within the time frame of the IANA Stewardship Transition. Work Stream 2 focuses on addressing accountability topics for which a timeline for developing solutions and full implementation may extend beyond the IANA Stewardship Transition.

Membership in the CCWG is open to individuals appointed by the various stakeholder organizations within the ICANN community. Decisions will be made by consensus. Additionally, the CCWG will be open to any interested person as a participant. Participants will be able to attend and participate in all meetings, but will not be part of any consensus or decisionmaking process.

Additionally, up to seven advisors, to be selected by a Public Experts Group,[23] will provide the CCWG with independent advice and research and identify best practices at an early stage of deliberation. Other members of the CCWG include an ICANN staff member, a past participant in the Accountability and Transparency Review Team(s), a liaison with the IANA Stewardship Transition Coordination Group (ICG), and an ICANN Board liaison. All of those individuals will participate but are not part of the decisionmaking process.

If approved by all or most of the CCWG chartering organizations, an accountability proposal will be submitted to the ICANN Board, which can approve the proposal or send it back to the CCWG for modification or reconsideration. Any decision by the Board not to implement a recommendation (or a portion of a recommendation) is to be accompanied by a detailed rationale.

The CCWG-Accountability group is comprised of 26 members appointed by chartering organizations and 150 participants contributing to mailing list conversations and meetings.[24]

Proposal

On August 3, 2015, the CCWG-Accountability group released its 2nd Draft Proposal containing Work Stream 1 recommendations.[25] The draft proposal recommended that ICANN be held accountable to the multistakeholder community by changing ICANN from a corporation with no members to a Sole Member Model which serves as a Community Mechanism in which ICANN's Supporting Organizations (SO) and Advisory Committees (AC)[26] jointly participate. No third parties and no individuals would become members of ICANN. Each decision would be made by the SOs and ACs through their own formal decision making processes, after a community-wide debate. Through this Community Mechanism, the multistakeholder community would be empowered to

- recall the entire ICANN Board of Directors;
- appoint and remove individual Board Directors;
- reconsider or reject the operating plan and budget;
- reconsider or reject changes to ICANN "Standard" Bylaws; and
- approve changes to "Fundamental" Bylaws.

Fundamental Bylaws offering special protections that preserve the multistakeholder community role would be established which could only be changed with 75% approval from the ICANN Board and prior approval by the multistakeholder community. The proposal also recommended incorporating the Affirmation of Commitments into the ICANN bylaws, enhancing ICANN's Independent Review Process, and reforming ICANN's Independent Review and Request for Reconsideration process.

The ICANN Board opposed the Sole Member model, arguing that it could destabilize the Board's ability to govern ICANN. At the ICANN54 Dublin meeting, the Board and the CCWG-Accountability group agreed to develop a revised proposal featuring a Sole Designator model for enforcing accountability.[27] Under the Sole Member model, the multistakeholder community would have the power to reconsider or reject ICANN's annual operating plan and budget. Under the Sole Designator model, the community would have recourse to recall Board members if it disagreed strongly enough with ICANN actions.

Stress Tests

A critical aspect of the CCWG-Accountability group proposal is designing "stress tests" for each solution or accountability measure that the two work streams develop. Stress tests are designed to measure the resistance of the accountability measures to various contingencies. The proposal has identified 37 specific contingencies that have been consolidated into five categories of stress tests:

- Financial crisis or insolvency: ICANN becomes fiscally insolvent, and lacks resources to adequately meet obligations;
- Failure to meet operational expectations: ICANN fails to process change or delegation requests to the IANA Root Zones, or executes a change of delegation over objections of stakeholders;
- Legal/legislative action: ICANN is the subject of litigation under existing or future policies, legislation, or regulation. ICANN attempts to delegate a new TLD or redelegate a non-compliant existing TLD;
- Failure of accountability: Action by one or more Board members, the CEO, or staff is contrary to mission or bylaws. ICANN is captured by one stakeholder segment; and
- Failure of accountability to external stakeholders: ICANN modifies its structure to avoid obligation to external stakeholders. ICANN delegates, subcontracts, or abdicates obligations to a third party. ICANN merges or is acquired by an unaccountable third party.[28]

According to the CCWG-Accountability charter, stress tests could include an analysis of potential weaknesses and risks; an analysis of existing remedies and their robustness; a definition of additional remedies or modification of existing remedies; and a description of how the proposed solutions would mitigate the risk of contingencies or protect the organization against such contingencies.[29]

Ultimately, any proposed accountability enhancements will be tested against the following questions:

- Do they make ICANN more susceptible to "capture" (or the assertion of undue influence) by one stakeholder or group of stakeholders?
- Can any individual or group make use of the redress and review processes in a way that paralyzes the work of ICANN?

- Does any group of stakeholders have the ability to modify its internal procedures in a way that shifts how it interacts among the rest of the stakeholders within ICANN?[30]

An issue surrounding stress tests regards Stress Test 18, which presents a scenario whereby the GAC amends their operating procedures to change from consensus decisions to majority voting for advice to ICANN's Board. Under current bylaws, ICANN must consider and respond to GAC advice, even if that advice is not supported by consensus. To address this, the CCWG recommended amending the bylaws to require trying to find a mutually acceptable solution only where GAC advice was supported by GAC consensus.

Timeline

After a comment period and feedback from multistakeholder groups, the CCWG-Accountability group plans to develop a revised proposal and submit its Work Stream 1 recommendations to the ICANN Board in late January 2016. This will be incorporated with the IANA transition proposal and submitted to NTIA, which will likely take two to three months to evaluate the proposal.[31] There will also likely be time allotted for Congress to evaluate the plan, and for the proposed transition actions to be fully tested and implemented. On August 17, 2015, NTIA announced that the IANA contract will be extended for one year until September 30, 2016.[32]

Role of NTIA

NTIA must approve the multistakeholder community proposal in order for the transition to take place. Given that Congress has prohibited NTIA from spending any FY2015 appropriated funds on relinquishing its responsibility with respect to Internet DNS functions, many observers wondered what role NTIA would play in the transition process during FY2015. At the 2015 State of the Net Conference, NTIA Administrator Lawrence Strickling stated:

> we will not use appropriated funds to terminate the IANA functions contract with ICANN prior to the contract's current expiration date of September 30, 2015. Nor will we use appropriated dollars to amend the

cooperative agreement with Verisign to eliminate NTIA's role in approving changes to the authoritative root zone file prior to September 30. On these points, there is no ambiguity.

The legislative language, however, makes it equally clear that Congress did not expect us to sit on the sidelines this year. The act imposes regular reporting requirements on NTIA to keep Congress apprised of the transition process. To meet those requirements, NTIA will actively monitor the discussions and activities within the multistakeholder community as it develops the transition plan. We will participate in meetings and discussions with ICANN, Verisign, other governments and the stakeholder community with respect to the transition. We will continue to represent the United States at the meetings of ICANN's Governmental Advisory Committee.

We will provide informal feedback where appropriate. We are as aware as anyone that we should not do anything that interferes with an open and participatory multistakeholder process. We support a process where all ideas are welcome and where participants are able to test fully all transition options. Nonetheless, the community should proceed as if it has only one chance to get this right. Everyone has the responsibility to participate as they deem appropriate. If, by asking questions, we can ensure that the community develops a well-thought-out plan that answers all reasonable concerns, we will do so.[33]

Administrator Strickling called on the CWG-Stewardship group to equally consider all transition proposal models and to ensure that any new organizational structures created to replace NTIA's oversight of the IANA functions contract be itself accountable and not susceptible to inefficiencies and politicization. With respect to the accountability process (CCWG-Accountability), NTIA stated that

it is critical that this group conduct "stress testing" of proposed solutions to safeguard against future contingencies such as attempts to influence or take over ICANN—be it the Board, staff or any stakeholder group—that are not currently possible given its contract with NTIA. We also encourage this group to address questions such as how to remove or replace board members should stakeholders lose confidence in them and how to incorporate and improve current accountability tools like the reviews called for by the Affirmation of Commitments.[34]

Finally, NTIA has stated that both transition processes (IANA function stewardship and accountability) should remain in sync, and that NTIA will only consider a coordinated and complete transition plan. NTIA has stated:

> As for timing, both groups are aiming to deliver a transition plan to us in the summer. While September 2015 has been a target date, because that is when the base period of our contract with ICANN expires, we have the flexibility to extend the contract if the community needs more time to develop the best plan possible.[35]

On August 17, 2015, NTIA announced its intention to extend the IANA function contract for one year, until September 30, 2016. NTIA stated that beyond 2016, they have the option of extending the contract for an additional period of up to three years, if needed.[36] NTIA also announced that in March 2015, it asked ICANN and Verisign to develop a transition plan for managing the root zone file after the IANA transition. Currently, NTIA has a cooperative agreement with Verisign which designates NTIA as the Root Zone Administrator. Under a proposal developed by ICANN and Verisign, the IANA Functions Operator (currently ICANN and to be determined under the IANA transition) will have administrative authority over Verisign's operation of the root zone file.[37]

Role of Congress in the IANA Transition

Concerns have arisen in Congress over the proposed transition. Some Members argue that the transition requires additional scrutiny by Congress, while others question whether the transition should take place at all. While the U.S. government has no statutory authority over ICANN or the DNS, Congress does have legislative and budgetary authority over NTIA, which is seeking to relinquish its contractual authority over the IANA functions. As such, Congress is keenly monitoring the progress of the transition, primarily through congressional committees with jurisdiction over NTIA. These include the House Energy and Commerce Committee and the Senate Commerce, Science, and Transportation Committee. Additionally, the House and Senate Appropriations Committees—which determine and control NTIA's annual budget—could impact NTIA's ability to relinquish its existing authority over the IANA functions.

Legislative Activities in the 113th Congress

On March 27, 2014, Representative Shimkus introduced H.R. 4342, the Domain Openness Through Continued Oversight Matters (DOTCOM) Act. H.R. 4342 would have prohibited the NTIA from relinquishing responsibility over the Internet domain name system until GAO submits to Congress a report on the role of the NTIA with respect to such system. The report would have included a discussion and analysis of the advantages and disadvantages of the change and addressed the national security concerns raised by relinquishing U.S. oversight. It would also have required GAO to provide a definition of the term "multistakeholder model" as used by NTIA with respect to Internet policymaking and governance. H.R. 4342 was referred to the House Energy and Commerce Committee. On April 2, 2014, the Subcommittee on Communications and Technology held a hearing on the DOTCOM Act.[38] H.R. 4342 was approved by the House Energy and Commerce Committee on May 8, 2014. Subsequently on June 5, 2014, the House Energy and Commerce Committee requested that the GAO examine the Administration's proposal to transition NTIA's current authority over IANA to the multistakeholder Internet community.[39] On August 15, 2015, GAO released a report finding that NTIA had not yet developed a formal framework for evaluating the transition plan. GAO recommended that NTIA review existing frameworks for evaluation to help evaluate and document whether and how the transition proposal meets NTIA's core goals.[40]

On May 22, 2014, the text of the DOTCOM Act was offered by Representative Shimkus as an amendment to H.R. 4435, the National Defense Authorization Act for FY2015. During House consideration of H.R. 4435, the amendment was agreed to by a vote of 245-177. H.R. 4435 was passed by the House on May 22, 2014. The House Armed Services bill report accompanying H.R. 4435 (H.Rept. 113-446) stated the committee's belief that any new Internet governance structure should include protections for the Department of Defense-controlled .mil generic top level domain and its associated Internet protocol numbers. The committee also supported maintaining separation between the policymaking and technical operation of root-zone management functions.

On June 2, 2014, the Senate Armed Services Committee reported S. 2410, its version of the FY2015 National Defense Authorization Act. Section 1646 of S. 2410 ("Sense of Congress on the Future of the Internet and the .mil Top-Level Domain") stated that it is the sense of Congress that the Secretary of Defense should

> advise the President to transfer the remaining role of the United States Government in the functions of the Internet Assigned Numbers Authority to a global multi-stakeholder community only if the President is confident that the '.MIL' top-level domain and the Internet Protocol address numbers used exclusively by the Department of Defense for national security will remain exclusively used by the Department of Defense.

Section 1646 also directed DOD to take "all necessary steps to sustain the successful stewardship and good standing of the Internet root zone servers managed by components of the Department of Defense." In the report accompanying S. 2410 (S.Rept. 113-176), the committee urged DOD to

> seek an agreement through the IANA transition process, or in parallel to it, between the United States and the Internet Corporation for Assigned Names and Numbers and the rest of the global Internet stakeholders that the .mil domain will continue to be afforded the same generic top level domain status after the transition that it has always enjoyed, on a par with all other country-specific domains.

The Carl Levin and Howard P. "Buck" McKeon National Defense Authorization Act for Fiscal Year 2015 was signed by the President on December 16, 2014 (P.L. 113-235). The enacted law does not contain the DOTCOM Act provision contained in the House-passed version. Section 1639 of P.L. 113-235 ("Sense of Congress on the Future of the Internet and the .mil Top-Level Domain") states it is the sense of Congress that the Secretary of Defense should support the IANA transfer

> only if assurances are provided for the protection of the current status of legacy top-level domain names and Internet Protocol address numbers, particularly those used by the Department of Defense and the components of the United States Government for national security purposes; mechanisms are institutionalized to uphold and protect consensus-based decision making in the multi-stakeholder approach; and existing stress-testing scenarios of the accountability process of the multi-stakeholder model can be confidently shown to work transparently, securely, and efficiently to maintain a free, open, and resilient Internet.

It is also the sense of Congress that the Secretary of Defense should "take all necessary steps to sustain the successful stewardship and good standing of the Internet root zone servers managed by components of the Department of

Legislative Activities in the 114th Congress

House Legislation

The DOTCOM Act of the 113th Congress was reintroduced into the 114th Congress by Representative Shimkus as H.R. 805 on February 5, 2015. As introduced, the DOTCOM Act of 2015 would have prohibited NTIA from relinquishing responsibility over the Internet domain name system until GAO submitted a report to Congress examining the implications of the proposed transfer. H.R. 805 would have directed GAO to issue the report no later than one year after NTIA received a transition proposal. On June 17, 2015, the House Committee on Energy and Commerce approved an amended DOTCOM Act. The amended version of H.R. 805 reflected a bipartisan agreement and was approved unanimously by voice vote. On June 23, 2015, H.R. 805 was passed by the House (378-25) under suspension of the rules.

H.R. 805, as passed by the House, does not permit NTIA's authority over the IANA function "to terminate, lapse, be cancelled, or otherwise cease to be in effect" until 30 legislative days after NTIA submits a report to Congress on the final IANA transition proposal. Specifically, the report must contain the final transition proposal and a certification by NTIA that the proposal

- supports and enhances the multistakeholder model of Internet governance;
- maintains the security, stability, and resiliency of the Internet domain name system;
- meets the needs and expectations of the global customers and partners of IANA services;
- maintains the openness of the Internet; and
- does not replace the role of NTIA with a government-led or intergovernmental organization solution.

H.R. 805 also requires NTIA to certify that the required changes to ICANN's bylaws contained in the transition proposal have been adopted by ICANN.

Meanwhile, on June 3, 2015, the House passed H.R. 2578, the FY2016 Commerce, Justice, Science (CJS) Appropriations Act, which appropriates funds for DOC and NTIA. Sec. 536 of H.R. 2578 states that "[n]one of the funds made available by this Act may be used to relinquish the responsibility of the National Telecommunications and Information Administration with respect to Internet domain name system functions, including responsibility with respect to the authoritative root zone file and the Internet Assigned Numbers Authority functions."

Other House-introduced legislation that addresses the proposed IANA transition includes

- H.R. 355 (Global Internet Freedom Act of 2015, introduced by Representative Duffy on January 14, 2015), which would prohibit NTIA from relinquishing its authority over the IANA functions.
- H.R. 2251 (Defending Internet Freedom Act of 2015, introduced by Representative Mike Kelly on May 15, 2015), which would prohibit NTIA from relinquishing its responsibilities over domain name functions and the IANA function unless it certifies that the transition proposal meets certain specified criteria.

Senate Legislation

S. 1551, the Senate companion version of the DOTCOM Act of 2015, was introduced on June 11, 2015 by Senator Thune. The language of S. 1551 is virtually identical to H.R. 805 as approved by the House Committee on Energy and Commerce. S. 1551 was referred to the Senate Committee on Commerce, Science, and Transportation.

On June 16, 2015, the Senate Appropriations Committee reported its version of the FY2016 Commerce, Justice, Science, and Related Agencies Appropriations Act. In the bill report (S.Rept. 114-66) the committee directed NTIA to "continue quarterly reports to the committee on all aspects of the transition process, and further directs NTIA to inform the Committee and the Senate Committee on Commerce, Science and Transportation, not less than 45 days in advance of any decision with respect to a successor contract." The committee also stated that it "continues to be concerned about this process and supports the continued stewardship role of the United States over the domain name system in order to ensure the security of the .gov and .mil domains and to protect the freedom of speech and expression internationally."

Also in the Senate, S.Res. 71—designating the week of February 8 through February 14, 2015, as "Internet Governance Awareness Week"—was introduced by Senator Hatch on February 5, 2015.

S.Res. 71 seeks to increase public awareness regarding NTIA's proposed transition, encourage public education about the importance of the transition process; and call the attention of the participants at the ICANN meeting in Singapore to the importance of designing accountability and governance reforms to best prepare ICANN for executing the responsibilities that it may receive under any transition of the stewardship of the IANA functions. S.Res. 71 was passed by the Senate on February 5, 2015.

Congressional Hearings

As part of its continuing oversight over NTIA and the domain name system, Congress has held hearings on the proposed IANA transition and on ICANN's management of the domain name system:

- On February 25, 2015, the Senate Committee on Commerce, Science, and Transportation held a hearing entitled, "Preserving the Multistakeholder Model of Internet Governance."[42]
- On May 13, 2015, the House Committee on Energy and Commerce, Subcommittee on Communications and Technology, held a hearing entitled, "Stakeholder Perspectives on the IANA Transition."[43]
- On May 13, 2015, the House Committee on the Judiciary, Subcommittee on Courts, Intellectual, Property and the Internet, held a hearing entitled, "Stakeholder Perspectives on ICANN: The .Sucks Domain and Essential Steps to Guarantee Trust and Accountability in the Internet's Operation."[44]
- On July 8, 2015, the House Committee on Energy and Commerce, Subcommittee on Communications and Technology, held a hearing entitled, "Internet Governance Progress After ICANN 53."[45]

Other Activities

On September 22, 2015, the Chairmen of the House and Senate Judiciary Committees (Representatives Goodlatte and Senator Grassley), Senator Cruz, and Representative Issa sent a letter to GAO expressing concern that the IANA transition and the relinquishing of U.S. government control over the root zone file may constitute a transfer of government property that may only be authorized by an act of Congress.[46] Specifically, the letter asked GAO to examine three questions: would the termination of NTIA's contract with ICANN cause government property of any kind to be transferred to ICANN; is the root zone file or other related of similar materials or information U.S. government property; and if so, does NTIA have the authority to transfer the root zone file or other related materials or information to a non-federal entity?

On October 15, 2015, the Chairman of the Senate Committee on Commerce, Science, and Transportation and the Ranking Member of the Subcommittee on Communications, Technology, Innovation, and the Internet

(Senator Thune and Senator Schatz) sent a letter[47] to ICANN calling for robust accountability reforms which may lessen the Board's power and authority if those reforms conform with the multistakeholder community's accountability proposal. The Senators further stated that no arbitrary deadlines should be used as a way to deter the community from securing the reforms it must have to sufficiently replace the role currently played by NTIA.

Key Issues for Congress

If the transition occurs and NTIA relinquishes its authority over the IANA functions, the U.S. government, through NTIA, will continue to participate in ICANN through the Governmental Advisory Committee. However, in a post-transition environment, the U.S. government (both the executive branch and Congress) will arguably have less authority and influence over ICANN and the DNS than it currently has.

Key issues for Congress are: should the NTIA relinquish its authority? If so, what organizational structures and safeguards should be in place within the multistakeholder transition plan to ensure that the domain name system remains stable, efficient, and free from the disproportionate influence of intergovernmental entities (such as the United Nations) as well as from other governments who may be hostile to U.S. interests?

Should the NTIA Relinquish Its Authority?

Supporters of the transition[48] argue that by transferring its remaining authority over ICANN and the DNS to the global Internet community, the U.S. government will bolster its continuing support for the multistakeholder model of Internet governance, and that this will enable the United States to more effectively argue and work against proposals for intergovernmental control over the Internet. The argument follows that if NTIA does *not* relinquish authority over the IANA functions, the United States will continue to be in the paradoxical and problematic position of opposing moves in intergovernmental fora to increase the power of governments in governing the Internet, while at the same time maintaining its unilateral authority over the Internet DNS by virtue of the IANA contract.

Supporters of the transition also point out that the U.S. government and Internet stakeholders have, from the inception of ICANN, envisioned that U.S. authority over IANA functions would be temporary, and that the DNS would eventually be completely privatized.[49] According to NTIA, this transition is now possible, given that "ICANN as an organization has matured and taken steps in recent years to improve its accountability and transparency and its technical competence."[50]

Those opposed, skeptical, or highly cautious about the transition[51] point out that NTIA's role has served as a necessary "backstop" to ICANN, which has given Internet stakeholders confidence that the integrity and stability of the DNS is being sufficiently overseen. Critics assert that in the wake of the Edward Snowden NSA revelations, foreign governments might gain more support internationally in their continuing attempts to exert intergovernmental control over the Internet, and that any added intergovernmental influence over the Internet and the DNS would be that much more detrimental to the interests of the United States if NTIA's authority over ICANN and the DNS were to no longer exist.

Another concern regards the development of the transition plan and a new international multistakeholder entity that would provide some level of stewardship over the DNS. Critics are concerned about the risks of foreign governments—particularly repressive regimes that favor censorship of the Internet—gaining influence over the DNS through the transition to a new Internet governance mechanism that no longer is subject to U.S. government oversight.

Transition Plan: External or Internal Solution?

NTIA and Congress will be examining whatever final transition plan is developed by the multistakeholder process. In the absence of NTIA's stewardship role (by virtue of the IANA functions contract with ICANN) will there be sufficient accountability checks on ICANN and the DNS? In other words, what entity or mechanism will assume NTIA's role after NTIA relinquishes its authority over the IANA function and its stewardship over ICANN?

A key issue is: to what extent should the proposed transition be addressed by an "external" or "internal" solution? Alternately, a hybrid solution could be developed which combines elements of both an external and internal approach. Under an external solution, a new organizational entity—controlled by Internet multistakeholders—would be formed to assume NTIA's oversight and stewardship role. The advantage of an external solution is "separability," whereby authority over the IANA functions would continue to be separated from ICANN, which sets DNS policy and currently acts as the IANA functions operator subject to its contract with NTIA. A separate entity with authority over the IANA functions could provide an accountability check on

ICANN similar to the accountability check that NTIA currently provides through the IANA functions contract. On the other hand, the disadvantage of an external solution is that creating new organizational entities and structures risks adding bureaucracy, inefficiency, politicization, and perhaps instability to the DNS.

Under an internal solution, authority over the IANA function would be transferred to ICANN itself. However, enhanced accountability measures would be put in place to ensure that ICANN remains accountable to the multistakeholder community, with internal mechanisms existing to enable multistakeholders to transfer authority over the IANA functions to another entity, if warranted. The advantage of an internal solution is that it would avoid the risks and possible dislocations of creating new organizational structures to oversee the IANA function (particularly domain name root zone oversight). The disadvantage is that an internal solution puts ICANN in the position of policing itself with respect to the IANA function, and some observers question whether internal accountability measures will be sufficient to ensure adequate stewardship over ICANN by the multistakeholder community.

Whether an external, internal, or hybrid solution is ultimately chosen, it is clear that ICANN's accountability and the authority over the IANA functions are inextricably linked. The two parallel multistakeholder processes—IANA stewardship transition and enhancing accountability—must be carefully coordinated, and the final transition proposal will be an integration of the results of both processes.

Concluding Observations

Ultimately, the debate over the transition will come down to the final transition proposal that is delivered to NTIA by the multistakeholder community. Stress tests—whereby the transition proposal is tested under various dire hypothetical scenarios—may be critically important to help NTIA and Congress evaluate the robustness of the transition plan.

The future of how ICANN and the DNS will be governed is highly relevant to the broader question of how the Internet should be governed. While it is true that ICANN's jurisdiction is limited to the technical underpinnings of the Internet (unique Internet identifiers such as domain names and addresses), it is also true that ICANN policy decisions (such new gTLDs) can affect other areas of Internet policy such as intellectual property, cybersecurity, privacy, and Internet freedom.

As the Internet expands and becomes more pervasive in all aspects of modern society, the question of how it should be governed becomes more pressing, with national governments recognizing an increasing stake in ICANN policy decisions, especially in cases where Internet DNS policy intersects with national laws and interests. While ICANN does not "control" the Internet, how it is ultimately governed may set an important precedent in future policy debates— both domestically and internationally—over how the Internet might be governed, and what role governments and intergovernmental organizations should play.

APPENDIX. ACRONYMS

Table A-1. Selected Acronyms Used in This Report

AoC	Affirmation of Commitments
CWG	Cross Community Working Group on Naming Related Functions
CCWG	Accountability Cross Community Working Group
DNS	domain name system
DOC	Department of Commerce
DOD	Department of Defense
GAC	Governmental Advisory Committee
GAO	Government Accountability Office
gTLD	generic top level domain
IAB	Internet Architecture Board
IANA	Internet Assigned Numbers Authority
ICANN	Internet Corporation for Assigned Names and Numbers
ICG	IANA Stewardship Transition Coordination Group
IETF	Internet Engineering Task Force
IP	Internet protocol
ISOC	Internet Society
NTIA	National Telecommunications Information Administration
PEG	Public Experts Group
PTI	post-transition IANA
RIRs	Regional Internet Registries

End Notes

[1] For more information on how the Internet is governed, see CRS Report R42351, Internet Governance and the Domain Name System: Issues for Congress, by Lennard G. Kruger.

[2] For a history of U.S. government involvement in the development of the Internet DNS, see ICANN Security and Stability Advisory Committee (SSAC), Overview and History of the IANA Functions, August 15, 2014, pp. 6-10, available at https://www.icann.org/en/system/files/files/sac-067-en.pdf. Also see Aaron Shull, Paul Twomey and Christopher S. Yoo, Global Commission on Internet Governance, Legal Mechanisms for Governing the Transition of Key Domain Name Functions to the Global Multi-stakeholder Community, November 2014, pp. 6-7, available at https://ourinternet-files.s3.amazonaws.com/publications/gcig_paper_no3.pdf.

[3] For more information on ICANN, see CRS Report 97-868, Internet Domain Names: Background and Policy Issues, by Lennard G. Kruger.

[4] The agreements between NTIA and ICANN are available at http://www.ntia.doc.gov/page/docicann-agreements.

[5] Internet Assigned Numbers Authority. See http://www.internetassignednumbersauthority.org/about.

[6] The authoritative root zone is a globally shared set of data that functions as a central and unified directory that ensures an Internet user will connect with the website that corresponds with the domain name that he or she types into their browser.

[7] According to the National Research Council, "The root zone file defines the DNS. For all practical purposes, a top level domain (and, therefore, all of its lower-level domains) is in the DNS if and only if it is listed in the root zone file. Therefore, presence in the root determines which DNS domains are available on the Internet." See National Research Council, Committee on Internet Navigation and the Domain Name System, Technical Alternatives and Policy Implications, Signposts on Cyberspace: The Domain Name System and Internet Navigation, National Academy Press, Washington, DC, 2005, p. 97.

[8] On August 17, 2015, NTIA announced that Verisign and ICANN had developed a proposal for removing NTIA's administrative role associated with root zone management as part of the IANA stewardship transition. See http://www.ntia.doc.gov/files/ntia/publications/root_zone_administrator_proposal-relatedtoiana_functionsste-final.pdf.

[9] An explanation of NTIA's role in managing the authoritative root zone file is at http://www.ntia.doc.gov/files/ntia/publications/ntias_role_root_zone_management_12162014.pdf.

[10] For more information on the GAC, see https://gacweb.icann.org/display/gacweb/Governmental+Advisory+Committee.

[11] NTIA, Press Release, "NTIA Announced Intent to Transition Key Internet Domain Name Functions," March 14, 2014, available at http://www.ntia.doc.gov/press-release/2014/ntia-announces-intent-transition-key-internet-domainname-functions.

[12] ICANN, "Montevideo Statement on the Future of Internet Cooperation," October 7, 2013, available at https://www.icann.org/en/news/announcements/announcement-07oct13-en.htm.

[13] Testimony of Lawrence Strickling, Assistant Secretary for Communications and Information, National Telecommunications and Information Administration, before the Senate Committee on Commerce, Science, and Transportation, "Preserving the Multistakeholder Model of Internet Governance," February 25, 2015, p. 11, available at http://www.commerce.senate.gov/public/?a=Files.Serve&File_id=3abbe751-4440-4c5f-83bd-382b38cbdc05.

[14] ICANN, "ICANN Board Statement on ICANN Sending IANA Stewardship Transition and Enhancing ICANN Accountability Proposals to NTIA," February 12, 2015, available at https://www.icann.org/news/announcement-3- 2015-02-12-en.

[15] Available at http://www.icann.org/en/about/agreements/iana/transition/draft-proposal-08apr14-en.htm.

[16] Ibid.

[17] Details on the Coordination Group are available at https://www.icann.org/resources/pages/process-next-steps-2014- 06-06-en#/.

[18] Information on ICG membership is available at https://www.icann.org/resources/pages/icg-members-2014-07-29-en.

[19] Charter for the IANA Stewardship Transition Coordination Group, August 27, 2014, available at https://www.icann.org/en/system/files/files/charter-icg-27aug14-en.pdf.

[20] Available at https://www.ianacg.org/icg-files/documents/IANA-transition-proposal-v9.pdf.

[21] ICANN Blog, "ICG Completes Its Work and Awaits Conclusion of CCWG on Enhancing ICANN Accountability," October 29, 2015, available at https://www.icann.org/news/announcement-2015-10-29-en.

[22] The CCWG Charter uses the following definition of stakeholder: "a person, group or organization that has a direct or indirect stake or interest in the organization because it can either affect the organization or be affected by it." See https://www.icann.org/news/announcement-2014-11-05-en.

[23] https://www.icann.org/news/announcement-2014-08-19-en.

[24] The latest statistics are available at https://community.icann.org/pages/viewpage.action?pageId=50823970.

[25] Available at https://www.icann.org/en/system/files/files/ccwg-draft-2-proposal-work-stream-1-recs-03aug15-en.pdf.

[26] For information on ICANN's Supporting Organizations and Advisory Committees, see https://www.icann.org/community#groups.

[27] ICANN Blog, "Cross Community Working Group on Enhancing ICANN Accountability ICANN54 Co-Chairs' Statement," October 22, 2015, available at https://www.icann.org/news/blog/cross-community-working-group-onenhancing-icann-accountability-icann54-co-chairs-statement.

[28] Cross Community Working Group on Enhancing ICANN Accountability (CCWG-Accountability),"Enhancing ICANN Accountability," February 11, 2015, p. 8, available at http://singapore52.icann.org/en/schedule/wed-ccwgaccountability/presentation-ccwg-accountability-11feb15-en.

[29] Cross Community Working Group (CCWG) Charter, November 3, 2014, p. 4, available at https://community.icann.org/display/acctcrosscomm/Charter.

[30] ICANN, Response to Question for the Record submitted by Senator Klobuchar, Senate Commerce Committee Hearing, "Preserving the Multistakeholder Model of Internet Governance," February 25, 2015, available at https://www.icann.org/en/system/files/correspondence/chehade-to-klobuchar-06apr15-en.pdf.

[31] Testimony available at http://energycommerce.house.gov/hearing/internet-governance-progress-after-icann-53.

[32] NTIA Administrator Lawrence E. Strickling, Blog, "An Update on the IANA Transition," August 17, 2015, available at http://www.ntia.doc.gov/blog/2015/update-iana-transition.

[33] NTIA, "Remarks by Assistant Secretary Strickling at the State of the Net Conference," January 27, 2015, available at http://www.ntia.doc.gov/speechtestimony/2015/remarks-assistant-secretary-strickling-state-net-conference-1272015.

[34] Ibid.

[35] NTIA, "Stakeholders Continue Historic Work on Internet DNS Transition at ICANN Singapore Meeting," February 19, 2015, available at http://www.ntia.doc.gov/blog/2015/stakeholders-continue-historic-work-internet-dns-transitionicann-singapore-meeting.

[36] NTIA Administrator Lawrence E. Strickling, Blog, "An Update on the IANA Transition," August 17, 2015, available at http://www.ntia.doc.gov/blog/2015/update-iana-transition.

[37] Verisign/ICANN Proposal in Response to NTIA Request: Root Zone Administrator Proposal Related to the IANA Functions Stewardship Transition, available at http://www.ntia.doc.gov/files/ntia/publications/root_zone_administrator_proposal-relatedtoiana_functionsste-final.pdf.

[38] Hearing before the House Energy and Commerce Committee, Subcommittee on Communications and Technology, "Ensuring the Security, Stability, Resilience, and Freedom of the Global Internet," April 2, 2014, available at http://energycommerce.house.gov/hearing/ensuring-security-stability-resilience-and-freedom-global-internet.

[39] See http://energycommerce.house.gov/sites/republicans.energycommerce.house.gov/files/letters/20140605GAO.pdf.

[40] Government Accountability Office, Internet Management: Structured Evaluation Could Help Assess Proposed Transition of Key Domain Name and Other Technical Functions, GAO-15-642, August 2015, 60 pages, available at http://www.gao.gov/assets/680/672055.pdf.

[41] House Subcommittee on Courts, Intellectual Property, and the Internet, Committee on the Judiciary, Hearing, "Should the Department of Commerce Relinquish Direct Oversight over ICANN?" April 10, 2014, testimony available at http://judiciary. house.gov/index.cfm/hearings?ID=027833A0-0028-42E2-A14B-B9C8BA2576A6.

[42] Testimony available at http://www.commerce.senate.gov/public/index.cfm?p=Hearings.

[43] Testimony available at http://energycommerce.house.gov/hearing/stakeholder-perspectives-iana-transition.

[44] Testimony available at http://judiciary.house.gov/index.cfm/hearings?ID=7E5AF16E-B1F8-45B8-803B9E389A9B745E.

[45] Testimony available at http://energycommerce.house.gov/hearing/internet-governance-progress-after-icann-53.

[46] Available at http://www.cruz.senate.gov/files/documents/Letters/20150922% 20Grassley%20Cruz%20Goodlatte%20Issa%20GAO%20Request%20ICANN.pdf.

[47] Available at https://regmedia.co.uk/2015/10/16/thune-schatz-icann-oct15.pdf.

[48] ICANN, "Endorsements of the IANA Globalization Process," March 18, 2014, available at https://www.icann.org/en/about/agreements/iana/globalization-endorsements-18mar14-en.pdf.

[49] The Commerce Department's June 10, 1998 Statement of Policy stated that the U.S. government "is committed to a transition that will allow the private sector to take leadership for DNS management." Available at http://www.ntia.doc.gov/legacy/ntiahome/domain name/6_5_98dns.htm.

[50] NTIA, Press Release, "NTIA Announced Intent to Transition Key Internet Domain Name Functions," March 14, 2014

[51] See for example, Atkinson, Rob, "U.S. Giving Up Its Internet 'Bodyguard' Role," March 17, 2014, available at http://www.ideaslaboratory.com/2014/03/17/u-s-giving-up-its-internet-bodyguard-role/; and Nagesh, Gauthem, Wall Street Journal, "U.S. Plan for Web Faces Credibility Issue," March 18, 2014.

In: Internet Governance
Editor: Ernestine Saunders

ISBN: 978-1-63484-920-3

Chapter 3

INTERNET MANAGEMENT: STRUCTURED EVALUATION COULD HELP ASSESS PROPOSED TRANSITION OF KEY DOMAIN NAME AND OTHER TECHNICAL FUNCTIONS*

United States Government Accountability Office

WHY GAO DID THIS STUDY

The U.S. government helped to fund the development of the Internet but since 1997 has envisioned that the coordination of certain Internet technical functions would be managed completely by the private sector. As the Internet has grown, the Department of Commerce's NTIA has contracted with a nonprofit corporation, ICANN, for the operation of these technical functions. In March 2014, NTIA established core goals for a transition proposal and announced that if a suitable proposal could be developed, NTIA would let the technical functions contract expire and transition its oversight role to a global multistakeholder community.

GAO was asked to review implications of NTIA's proposed transition. This report examines: (1) the process of developing a transition proposal and addressing identified transition risks, and (2) NTIA's plans to evaluate a proposal. GAO reviewed NTIA's evaluation plans and identified frameworks

---

* This is an edited, reformatted and augmented version of the United States Government Accountability Office publication, GAO-15-642, dated August 2015.

for NTIA to use in its evaluation; reviewed transition documents; and interviewed officials from NTIA, other federal agencies assisting NTIA with the proposed transition, and ICANN, as well as stakeholders selected based on their technical, commercial, and academic backgrounds.

What GAO Recommends

GAO recommends that NTIA review relevant frameworks for evaluation and use applicable portions to help evaluate the transition proposal. The Department of Commerce concurred with the recommendation.

What GAO Found

The National Telecommunications and Information Administration (NTIA) announced that it would transition its oversight of the coordination of certain key Internet technical functions (such as the domain name system) to the global multistakeholder community if a suitable transition proposal were developed. In response, several steps were taken to develop a proposal and address identified risks. The Internet Corporation for Assigned Names and Numbers (ICANN), which operates these technical functions under contract with NTIA, convened stakeholders from technical, government, business, and public interest organizations, among others. These stakeholders formed working groups with the goal to develop a consensus-based proposal they plan to provide to the ICANN board by late fall 2015. The board will then provide the proposal to NTIA. In draft proposals, working groups have proposed new post-transition arrangements to manage identified risks and hold ICANN accountable to the multistakeholder community. For example, stakeholders identified a risk that ICANN could be captured by a particular interest. To address this risk, stakeholders proposed changes that would empower the multistakeholder community to veto board decisions related to ICANN's plans and budget and to remove board members, among other things.

NTIA plans to evaluate the proposal against core goals, such as maintaining the security and stability of the Internet domain name system and the openness of the Internet. However, NTIA has not yet determined how it will evaluate the proposal against the goals. The changes the working groups are considering could create a new organizational environment for the operation of the technical functions, such as new structures, contractual obligations, and governance models for ICANN. Given the extent of these potential changes, GAO identified frameworks for evaluation that could provide tools to guide NTIA's evaluation.

- These frameworks incorporate leading practices to help organizations obtain reasonable assurance that their goals and objectives will be met or that they will meet certain requirements. For example, key components of one framework include the organizational environment, risk assessment, and monitoring.
- In prior work, GAO has considered such frameworks in relationship to accountability challenges at a variety of organizations. These types of frameworks could help NTIA evaluate whether the transition proposal meets its core goals, and could also be helpful in considering accountability mechanisms that are included in the proposal. For example, one framework's risk assessment component could help NTIA consider the multistakeholder community's efforts to identify and manage risks.
- These frameworks are intentionally flexible, so that NTIA could select elements that are applicable to the scope of the proposed transition.

Without a framework as a tool to systematically review the proposal and its various new structures and processes, NTIA may not be assured that its goals for the transition have been fully addressed and embedded over the long term.

ABBREVIATIONS

COSO	Committee of Sponsoring Organizations of the Treadway Commission
COSO framework	Committee of Sponsoring Organizations of the Treadway Commission Internal Control—Integrated Framework
FirstNet	First Responder Network Authority
IANA	Internet Assigned Numbers Authority
ICANN	Internet Corporation for Assigned Names and Numbers
IETF	Internet Engineering Task Force

IP	Internet Protocol
ISO	International Organization for Standardization
ITU	International Telecommunication Union
NIST	National Institute of Standards and Technology
NTIA	National Telecommunications and Information Administration
RFC	request for comment
RIR	regional Internet registries

***

August 19, 2015

Congressional Requesters

The Internet has evolved from a research project involving four host computers in the 1960s to a vast global system of interconnected networks used by billions of people across the world to perform personal, educational, commercial, and governmental tasks.[1] The central coordination of certain technical functions related to maintaining unique identifiers (such as the domain name system) helps computers communicate over the Internet.[2] For example, each device that connects to the Internet has a unique identifying number—an Internet Protocol (IP) address—so that information can be sent to or received from a specific device. Use of the Internet has expanded so rapidly that one set of IP addresses, which was developed in the early 1980s and which provided approximately 4 billion addresses, was not sufficient to accommodate the growing number of users and devices.[3] To accommodate the expected continued expansion of the Internet, the next generation of IP addresses was developed to include up to 340 undecillion (340×10^{36}) addresses—more than a trillion IP addresses for each person in the world.

The U.S. government played a role in funding the development of the early Internet.[4] In 1997, the President directed the Secretary of Commerce to move the governance of the domain name system into the private sector to increase competition and promote international participation.[5] After the Department of Commerce's National Telecommunications and Information Administration (NTIA)[6] issued a 1998 policy statement,[7] the Internet Corporation for Assigned Names and Numbers (ICANN) was formed as a nonprofit to manage these technical functions for the benefit of the Internet community as a whole. The Department of Commerce subsequently entered into an agreement with ICANN to carry out these functions.[8] ICANN—a California-based, nonprofit corporation—currently operates these technical functions under a no-cost contract with NTIA.[9] ICANN has managed these technical functions through a governance model in which a multistakeholder community—interested parties from all over the world and from multiple sectors and industries, including technical, government, business, and public-interest organizations—develop policies that support how the Internet domain name system is operated. This model of Internet governance—referred to as the "multistakeholder model"—is a system of open, bottom-up, and participatory self-governance. NTIA has supported this type of bottom-up, private sector coordination since its 1998 policy statement.

In March 2014, NTIA announced that if a suitable plan could be formed, it would finalize the transition of these Internet technical functions to the multistakeholder community by letting its contract with ICANN expire, thus ending the U.S. government's role. In the announcement, NTIA included a list of core goals for the transition and asked ICANN to convene global stakeholders to develop a transition proposal. NTIA has stated that this proposal must meet its core goals and have the broad support of the multistakeholder community for NTIA to allow the contract to expire. The target date for the transition is September 2015, when the current contract expires, but NTIA may extend the contract for up to 4 years.[10]

NTIA and some stakeholders view the transition as an important sign of the U.S. government's following through on its endorsement of the multistakeholder model of Internet governance. Some stakeholders, however, have expressed concerns about potential risks related to the transition. You asked us to review the implications of the proposed transition. This report examines: (1) the process being used to develop a transition proposal and address risks related to the transition, as identified by stakeholders, and (2) NTIA's plans to evaluate a transition proposal against its core goals for the transition and additional tools for evaluation that could help NTIA with its assessment.

To respond to these objectives, we reviewed documents related to the Internet technical functions, NTIA, and ICANN. We interviewed technical experts from, among other organizations, the National Institute of Standards and Technology (NIST). We followed transition efforts, including observing multiple sessions at an ICANN meeting, listening to multistakeholder working group meetings, and reviewing relevant documents and draft proposals from transition working groups. We also compared the process used to develop the transition proposal to risk management principles. We reviewed NTIA's plans for evaluating the transition proposal and identified potential tools, including frameworks for evaluation, for NTIA to use in its evaluation. We selected these principles and frameworks based in part on our prior work. In addition to our risk management and internal controls frameworks, the other principles and frameworks we considered were designed by nongovernmental organizations—the Committee of Sponsoring Organizations of the Treadway Commission and the International Organization for Standardization—with the goal of improving risk management and organizational performance in a broad range of organizations. We interviewed and/or received written responses from stakeholders from NTIA and 10 other federal entities that play a role in Internet-related issues, including entities within the Departments of Defense, Homeland Security, Justice, and State; the General Services Administration; and the Federal Communications Commission. The majority of these entities were involved in an NTIA-convened interagency working group, according to NTIA. We also interviewed 31 nonfederal stakeholders, including ICANN's management, board chair, and one board member; chairs, members, or participants in ICANN's multistakeholder working groups for the transition; economists with knowledge about ICANN, and officials from industry groups and associations, Internet freedom organizations, businesses, telecommunications companies, think tanks, and academic institutions with a focus on Internet governance issues. The information from these interviews is not generalizable but provided us with a broad perspective from knowledgeable stakeholders on potential risks related to the transition and the multistake-holder community's approach to developing a transition proposal to address potential risks and meet NTIA's core goals. See appendix I for a more detailed description of our scope and methodology.

We conducted this performance audit from September 2014 to August 2015 in accordance with generally accepted government auditing standards. Those standards require that we plan and perform the audit to obtain sufficient, appropriate evidence to provide a reasonable basis for our findings and conclusions based on our audit objectives. We believe that the evidence obtained provides a reasonable basis for our findings and conclusions based on our audit objectives.

BACKGROUND

Internet Technical Functions

Certain technical functions make it possible for computers and other devices to share information across the Internet, as shown in Figure 1.[11] The developers of the Internet determined that centrally coordinating these technical functions would be the most efficient way to allow every device that is connected to the Internet to communicate with other devices—whether the network consisted of just a few computers as in the beginning—or the billions of devices that access the Internet today. These technical functions fall into three categories (see Figure 1):

- protocol parameters—unique values used in standards for formatting data so that information can be sent and received over a network,
- numbers—unique identifiers known as IP addresses that are assigned to each device on the Internet, and
- names—strings of text separated by dots, such as www.gao.gov. Domain names are mapped into IP addresses using a global domain name system.

Collectively, these functions became known as the Internet Assigned Numbers Authority (IANA) functions. Originally, the functions were provided by one person. Currently a department within ICANN operates these functions. ICANN's role in coordinating these functions involves maintaining lists of these protocol parameters, IP addresses, and top- level domains (such as .gov). NTIA has proposed transitioning its role related to these functions.

These technical functions are interdependent and support efficient communication among devices that connect to the Internet. Protocols define the format of information exchanged through the Internet and the commands to manage how devices send and receive that information. Using a common set of protocol parameters allows devices to communicate. Unique identifying numbers (IP addresses) are necessary to send that information from one device to another. Domain names equate to IP addresses and are used because it is easier for people to remember names than long strings of identifying numbers. Thus, the domain name system makes it easier for humans to navigate the

Internet. This system maps domain names into IP addresses, allowing an Internet user to access a website by typing a domain name (www.gao.gov) into a browser rather than the IP address (161.203.16.77). The domain name system is constructed as a hierarchy. In left-to-right languages like English, the top level is what appears at the far right of the domain name, after the last dot, as shown in Figure 2.

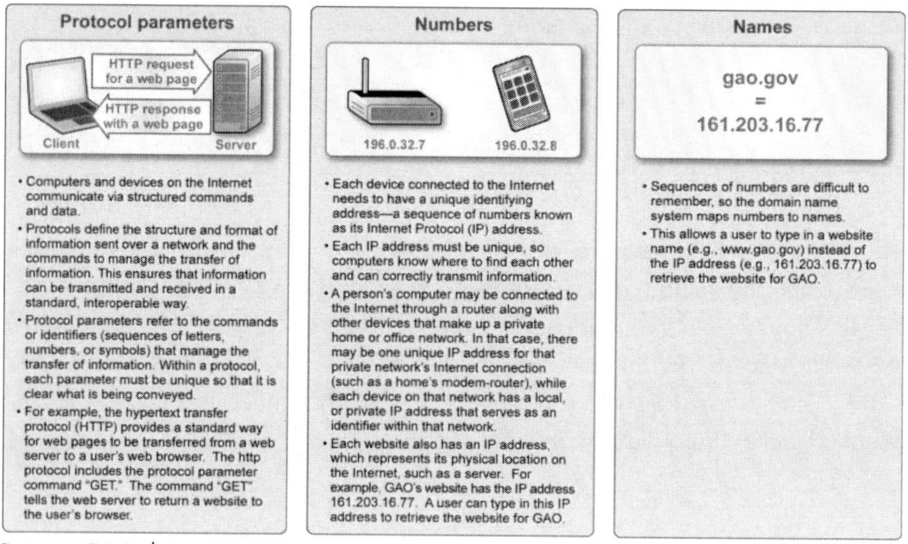

Source: GAO. | GAO-15-642

Figure 1. Illustration of How Certain Technical Functions Are Important to the Operation of the Internet.

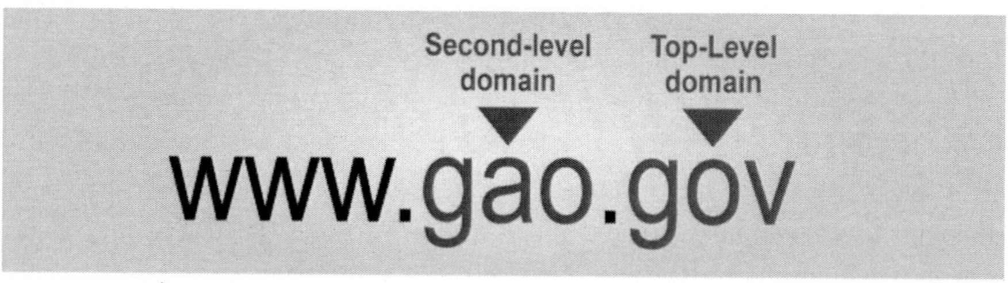

Source: GAO. | GAO-15-642

Figure 2. The Hierarchical Organization of Internet Domain Names.

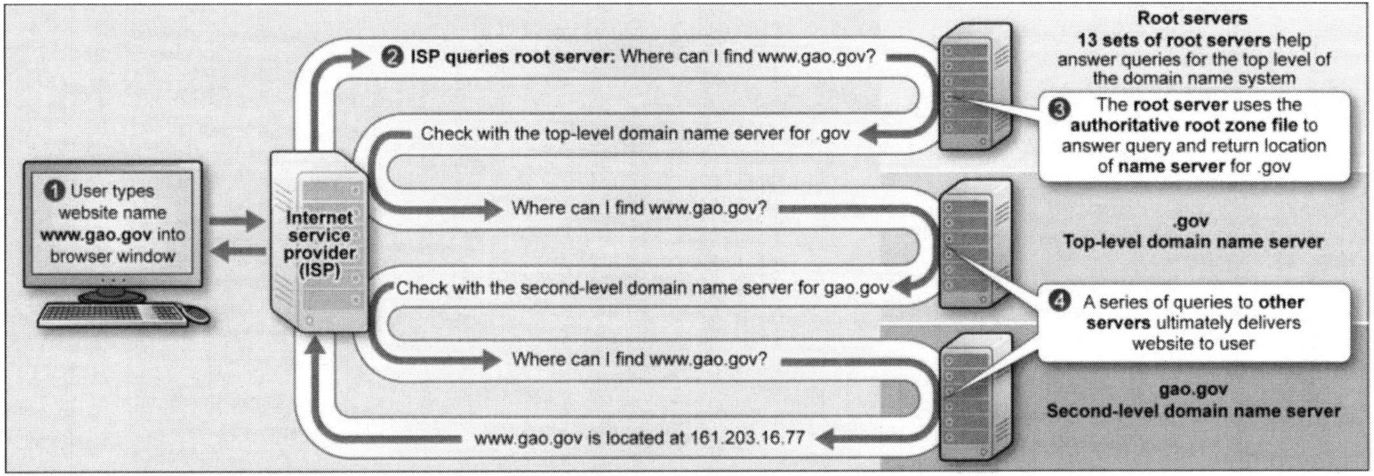

Source: GAO. | GAO-15-642

Figure 3. How the Domain Name System Uses the Authoritative Root Zone File to Direct an Internet Query.

Across the world, the domain name system has 13 sets of root servers, which form a network of hundreds of servers that play a central role in the Internet's system for finding a particular website. Each of these servers has a copy of a file called the authoritative root zone file, which is a type of "address book" for the top level (and only the top level) of the domain name system—listing, among other things, the IP addresses of all top- level domains' name servers. Generally, as shown in Figure 3, when a person using the Internet types a website (such as www.gao.gov) into his or her browser, this begins with a query to the person's Internet service provider for the IP address of that website. The Internet service provider then queries the domain name system for the IP address, as shown in Figure 3. This process can all take place within fractions of a second.

No formal institutional or governmental mechanism enforces the way the system works. Technical experts have explained that Internet users have adhered to the system of technical functions because it works for them, with the more people using the same system increasing the value for all those using the system. For example, while nothing stops any user from opting out of using the standard protocols, a computer that deviates from the standards risks losing the ability to communicate with other computers that do follow the standards. A user is also not required to use a uniquely assigned IP address, but using a unique address is necessary to enable other systems to send information to the appropriate recipient over the Internet. In addition, the entire system is distributed. That is, the Internet is a broad network of smaller networks operated by entities such as companies or universities. Technical structures that support the system are also distributed, such as the 13 sets of root zone servers that have copies of the authoritative root zone file.

ICANN's Duties as Technical Functions Operator: Protocol Parameters, Numbers, and Names

Under the terms of its contract with NTIA and a related agreement with another entity, ICANN performs certain Internet technical functions. ICANN's operation of these technical functions does not involve the content that appears on the Internet or who can connect to the Internet, according to ICANN. ICANN also has a role in coordinating Internet policy making, a role that we discuss later. According to ICANN, this policy- making role is not governed by ICANN's contract with NTIA.[12]

Protocol Parameters: ICANN maintains a complete and public database of protocol parameters—the unique identifiers for commands or types of data used in established protocols.[13] For example, while "GET" is a command in the HTTP protocol, as described in Figure 1, "TEXT" indicates that the type of data being transmitted is text. ICANN maintains the database of protocol parameters under a separate memorandum of understanding between ICANN and the Internet Engineering Task Force (IETF).[14] When a new protocol is established, such as a protocol for sending and receiving a new type of video file, ICANN adds the protocol parameters to the public database so that all software developers can easily access those parameters. According to this memorandum of understanding, ICANN's technical functions staff will generally assign and register protocol parameters as directed by criteria and procedures specified in request-for-comments documentation.[15] According to ICANN, its technical functions staff process more than 300 requests per month to add to or update the protocol parameter database.[16] Figure 4 shows how protocol parameters are developed, published, and accessed and used.

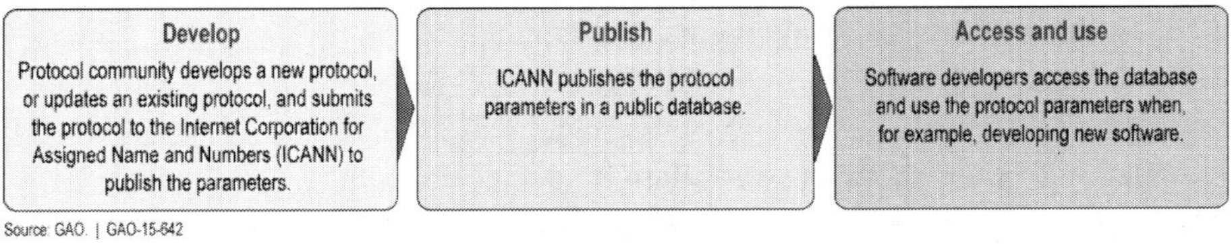

Source: GAO. | GAO-15-642

Figure 4. Internet Protocol Parameter Development, Publishing, and Access and Use.

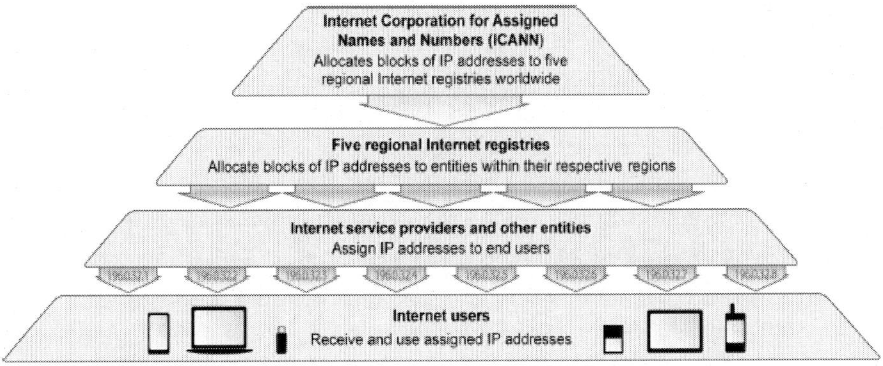

Source: GAO. | GAO-15-642

Figure 5. Allocation and Assignment of Internet Protocol (IP) Addresses.

Numbers: ICANN allocates large blocks of IP addresses and other numbers to the five regional Internet registries world-wide, according to globally developed policies.[17] This responsibility is defined by ICANN's contract with NTIA. (A separate memorandum of understanding between ICANN and the five regional Internet registries documents the global policy development process for the numbers community). Each regional Internet registry further allocates blocks of IP addresses in its particular region of the world.[18] These IP addresses eventually reach Internet service providers and end users. Figure 5 provides more detail about how these numbers are allocated and assigned.

Names: In concert with NTIA and a company called Verisign, with which NTIA has a separate cooperative agreement, ICANN processes changes to the top level of the domain name system (e.g., changes to the authoritative root zone file).[19] ICANN receives these change requests, checks that appropriate technical and policy requirements were followed, and then sends the request in parallel to NTIA for verification and authorization and to Verisign for implementation. (Verisign will not implement the request until authorized by NTIA.) After Verisign implements the change, it distributes the updated authoritative root zone file to the 13 sets of root servers. ICANN also maintains the root zone database, which lists the operators of all the top-level domains and their contact information.[20] Two examples of changes that ICANN processes as part of the names function include:

- Adding a new generic top-level domain.[21] Once a new top-level domain has been approved in a separate multistakeholder process, ICANN receives the request to add the associated information to the authoritative root zone file. As described above, ICANN checks that appropriate requirements were followed and then sends the proposed change to NTIA and Verisign. Processing these types of changes to the root zone file ensures that computers can look up information from the domain name system (e.g., IP addresses) for websites under that new generic top-level domain. (For example, on May 6, 2015, the new top level domain .theater was added to the authoritative root zone file.)
- Changing the IP address of a name server for a top-level domain, at the request of the registry (the company or organization that operates the top-level domain). For example, top-level domain registries may contract with other companies to host their name servers. If the registry changes contractors, the IP addresses of its name servers may

change as well. Keeping this information in the authoritative root zone file up to date is important so that queries using the top level of the domain name system can be directed properly.

NTIA's Role in the Technical Functions and Transition Announcement

NTIA has a contractual relationship with ICANN in which the parties have agreed that ICANN will carry out the IANA technical functions. The terms of the contract, as agreed to by NTIA and ICANN, specify the roles of ICANN related to the protocol parameters, numbers, and names functions. For example, the current contract specifies how ICANN should receive and process changes to the authoritative root zone file for the names function. At the expiration of the contract with ICANN, NTIA may decide whether it wishes to renew the contract with ICANN. When issuing a new solicitation for the technical functions, NTIA has exercised some discretion in deciding how the new IANA functions contract would be ultimately awarded. For example, based on the input received from stakeholders around the world, NTIA added new requirements to the contract's statement of work for the competitive-bidding process in 2011. NTIA noted in a public notice in 2012 that these new requirements included the need for a separation of policy making from implementation, a robust company-wide conflict-of-interest policy, provisions reflecting heightened respect for local country laws, and consultation and reporting to increase transparency and accountability to the international community. Initially, NTIA determined that no bid submitted met the requirements and canceled the bidding process, temporarily extending the contract with ICANN and deciding to reissue the request for proposal at a later date. After a new bidding process and submission by ICANN, NTIA awarded the most recent contract to ICANN in July 2012.

Under the contract, NTIA also has an operational role related to the names function in which it verifies and authorizes changes made to the top level of the domain name system.[22] NTIA verifies that ICANN followed established processes and procedures when submitting the proposed change to the authoritative root zone file, then authorizes Verisign to implement the change.[23]

On March 14, 2014, NTIA announced its intent to transition its role related to the Internet technical functions to the global multistakeholder community. As the first step, NTIA asked ICANN to convene global stakeholders to develop a proposal to transition the current role played by NTIA in the coordination of these functions. NTIA communicated to ICANN that it would only accept a transition proposal that has broad multistakeholder community support and addresses the following five core goals:

- support and enhance the multistakeholder model;
- maintain the security, stability, and resiliency of the Internet domain name system;
- meet the needs and expectations of the global customers and partners of the IANA services;
- maintain the openness of the Internet; and
- not replace NTIA's role with a government-led or an inter-governmental organization solution.

NTIA sees this transition as the final step of a process envisioned by the U.S. government since 1997, when a presidential memorandum directed the Secretary of Commerce to move the coordination of the technical functions out of the government sector, recognizing the importance of a market-oriented, global, and transparent approach to supporting the Internet's growth and increasingly commercial nature.[24]

ICANN's Governance and Policy Development

ICANN's mission, according to its bylaws, is to coordinate and ensure the stable and secure operation of the global Internet's systems of unique identifiers (the protocol parameters, numbers, and names functions, as described above). Its mission also includes coordinating policy development "reasonably and appropriately" related to these technical functions. For example, a major policy undertaking in recent years has been the consideration and establishment of the new generic top-level domain program, which ICANN launched in June 2011. While prior to the program, there were 22 generic top-level domains, as of April 3, 2015, 583 additional top-level domains had been introduced into the domain name system, with about 1,000 more in the process, according to ICANN officials.

ICANN is generally governed by a board of directors, which has final authority over policy decisions. The board consists of 16 voting members who, with the exception of the president of ICANN, are selected either by a nominating committee or the stakeholder groups described below. (For more detail about the board, see app. II). In line with its core value of seeking and supporting broad, informed participation reflecting the functional, geographic, and cultural diversity of the Internet at all levels of policy development and decision making, ICANN's bylaws specify a number of supporting organizations and advisory committees (see Figure 6). These supporting organizations and advisory committees provide the organizational structure through which those with interests and concerns related to Internet governance can interact with ICANN to develop policies related to the domain name system. Collectively, these individuals and organizations are a subset of the multistakeholder community that is involved in ICANN-related policy development and other activities. According to ICANN officials, the three supporting organizations each represent a particular area of ICANN's policy efforts and are responsible for presenting policy proposals to the board that have been developed through a bottom-up, consensus process. This process involves, among other things, various regional organizations and constituency groups that develop relevant policy initiatives.[25] The advisory committees provide advice and input to ICANN's board and the ICANN community as applicable to their expertise, and certain other technical bodies also provide advice.[26]

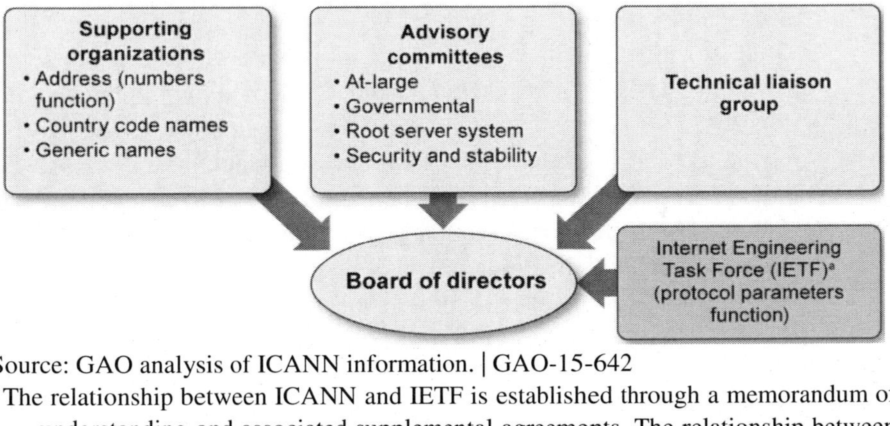

Source: GAO analysis of ICANN information. | GAO-15-642

[a] The relationship between ICANN and IETF is established through a memorandum of understanding and associated supplemental agreements. The relationship between ICANN's board and the other groups in this figure is established in ICANN's bylaws.

Figure 6. Multistakeholder Structure of the Internet Corporation for Assigned Names and Numbers (ICANN).

The policy development process is highly structured. First, a policy is developed according to the structured process defined for its relevant area. Once stakeholders in the relevant area reach a consensus proposal, the supporting organization presents the proposal to the board. Then the board must follow certain measures for considering the policy and has the final say in whether the policy is approved. ICANN officials told us that, combined, the supporting organizations and advisory committees are meant to ensure that the following groups of stakeholders, among others, are involved in developing ICANN's policies:

- the five regional Internet registries, which are responsible for allocating IP addresses within their global regions;
- country code top-level domain managers (i.e., companies or organizations that operate country-code top-level domains, such as .us, the top-level domain for the United States);
- generic top-level domain registries (companies or organizations that operate top-level domain names—such as .com and .org—that are not specified as country-codes);
- registrars, the companies that register domain names (frequently websites, such as www.example.com) to users;
- other commercial stakeholders, which include, for example, Internet-based companies (e.g., Google or Facebook), large and small businesses that use the Internet to sell products, Internet service providers, and various stakeholders concerned with intellectual property;
- noncommercial stakeholders, such as individuals and nonprofit organizations involved in research and education, or those that are concerned with human rights, consumer protection, and public interest aspects of domain name policy;
- governments (through the Governmental Advisory Committee);
- technical experts on specific Internet-related considerations (through the Root Server System Advisory Committee and the Security and Stability Advisory Committee); and
- individual Internet users (through the At-Large Advisory Committee).

From early on, ensuring ICANN's accountability to the multistakeholder community has been a key objective. In 2002, we testified that progress had been slow in creating sufficient processes to represent the functional and geographic diversity of the Internet, and for the use of private, bottom-up coordination rather than government control.[27] Since that time, ICANN has made a number of changes to its bylaws—including changes that affect the composition and selection of its board, to address these issues and enhance accountability. (For more on measures in ICANN's bylaws related to transparency and accountability and on the composition of its board, see app. II). In addition, in 2009, ICANN and NTIA, through the Department of Commerce, signed an affirmation of commitments to further enhance ICANN's accountability. Under this affirmation of commitments, ICANN will facilitate a series of community-led reviews of ICANN as an organization.[28] To date, two sets of accountability and transparency reviews have been undertaken and have covered topics such as ICANN's public comment process and the ICANN board's governance and performance. The ICANN board has accepted all of the recommendations from these reviews and is in the process of implementing them, with regular updates provided to the multistakeholder community on ICANN's public website. The affirmation of commitments, which is separate from NTIA's contract with ICANN, can be canceled by either party with 120 days' notice.[29]

In addition to operating these Internet technical functions and facilitating reasonably related policy development, ICANN holds contracts with and receives most of its revenue from:

- generic top-level domain registries (such as the company Verisign, which operates the top-level domains .com, .net, and .name), and
- registrars for generic top-level domains (such as the company GoDaddy, with whom a company or individual can go to register a new domain name, such as example.com).

ICANN also has agreements with some, but not all, country-code top-level domain managers.[30] According to ICANN, its arrangements with these country-code top-level domain managers are not as formalized and consistent as those with generic top-level domain registries. ICANN officials said that while some country-code top-level domain managers make payments to ICANN, these are considered voluntary contributions, in contrast to standard fees paid to ICANN by generic top-level domain registries. See appendix II for more information about the contractual relationships among parties in the generic domain name industry, along with fees paid to ICANN. Under their contracts with ICANN, top-level domain registries and domain name registrars must perform certain required functions or they can lose their accreditation, which would prevent them from doing business as a top-level domain registry or registrar. For example, registrars must record contact information for every entity that registers a domain name through them in what is known as the Whois service. Relevant policies developed through ICANN's multistakeholder policy development process and approved by ICANN's board automatically become incorporated into these contracts, so long as these changes do not constitute "restricted amendments" under the registrar agreements.

WORKING GROUPS ARE USING A MULTISTAKEHOLDER PROCESS TO DEVELOP A TRANSITION PROPOSAL AND HELP MANAGE IDENTIFIED RISKS

ICANN Convened Multistakeholder Working Groups to Develop a Transition Proposal

In response to NTIA's announcement asking ICANN to convene global stakeholders to develop a transition proposal that would meet NTIA's core goals, ICANN convened the multistakeholder community at its March 2014 public meeting in Singapore[31] to join ICANN in developing the transition process. Representatives from governments, the private sector, Internet organizations, and Internet users from around the world were invited to participate in meetings, either in-person or remotely, via streaming live audio and video, chatrooms, online question boxes, and e- mail—to provide input into the process to develop the transition proposal. This information was later compiled and incorporated into materials posted to ICANN's website on April 8, 2014, for a one-month public comment period.

On June 6, 2014, ICANN posted the process to develop the proposal and next steps.[32] ICANN envisioned that the process would be inclusive, consensus-based, transparent, and focused in scope, among other key principles. ICANN, based on input from the multistakeholder community, proposed using existing information and processes, multi-lingual support, and web-based platforms, among other mechanisms, to ensure an open, inclusive, transparent, and accountable process. At the multistakeholder community's request, a coordination group to oversee the transition proposal process was established.[33] In September 2014, the coordination group issued a request for proposals that asked each of the three communities with a direct operational relationship with ICANN in its role as operator of these technical functions—the protocol parameters, numbers, and names communities—to develop a transition proposal through a transparent process that is open to and inclusive of all interested stakeholders. In response, each of these three communities established a working group to develop a transition proposal. Initially, the coordination group developed a timeline that called for the final proposal to be submitted to NTIA before the expiration of the contract for these Internet technical functions on September 30, 2015; however, as explained below, this time frame was amended in July 2015.

The coordination group's request for proposals specified that the proposal from each of the three technical function communities—the protocol parameters, numbers, and names communities—should describe:

- The technical function involved.
- How current policies, oversight, and accountability are established under the existing arrangement, which includes the IANA functions contract between NTIA and ICANN.
- Any proposed changes to how policies, oversight, and accountability would be established in the absence of a contract between NTIA and ICANN.
- Transition implications, including risks to operational continuity and how they will be addressed.
- How the proposal meets NTIA's published core goals for the transition.
- How the process used to develop the proposal incorporates principles of community involvement, openness, and transparency, including the level of consensus achieved.

The coordination group stated that it would assess the proposals from the three technical function communities for compatibility and interoperability and assemble them into one complete proposal for the transition.

During discussions regarding how the three technical function working groups would develop the transition proposal, the multistakeholder community raised the broader topic of the effect of the transition on ICANN's accountability generally. At the request of participants of the multistakeholder community, an accountability working group was created to focus on ensuring that ICANN remains accountable in the absence of its historical contractual relationship with the U.S. government.[34] According to the accountability working group, this contractual relationship with the U.S. government has been perceived as a backstop with regard to ICANN's organization-wide accountability since 1998.

Each technical function working group[35] and the accountability working group created a charter that helped to guide its work. Each working group consists of chairs and members or participants from relevant parts of the multistakeholder community,[36] but any interested individual may observe meetings and contribute to discussions. The three technical working groups developed their proposals in line with the requirements laid out by the coordination group. The accountability working group followed a separate and parallel process to develop its draft proposal with the goal of identifying a broader set of reforms necessary to enhance ICANN's accountability towards the global multistakeholder community (see Figure 7).

Each group's process was intended to be open and inclusive, supported by stakeholders participating through face-to-face and virtual meetings open to the public in which elements of the draft proposals were discussed and revised, and public mailing lists were created to allow interested parties or individuals to participate in discussions and observe the process with the goal of developing a consensus proposal. The working groups' activities—including meeting proceedings and e-mail discussions, for example—were archived and have been made publicly available along with relevant documents.[37]

By the end of June 2015, all three technical function working groups had completed their draft proposals and submitted them to the coordination group for its review and comment. While the protocol parameters and numbers groups had completed their proposals earlier in 2015, the names working group submitted its proposal on June 25, 2015, after getting approval from all chartering organizations during ICANN's 53rd meeting in Buenos Aires. The coordination group then assembled the proposals into one complete draft proposal, which it posted on its website for a public comment period from July 31 through September 8, 2015. Once the public comments, if any, have been addressed, the coordination group plans to submit the final proposal to the ICANN board to transmit to NTIA within 14 days.

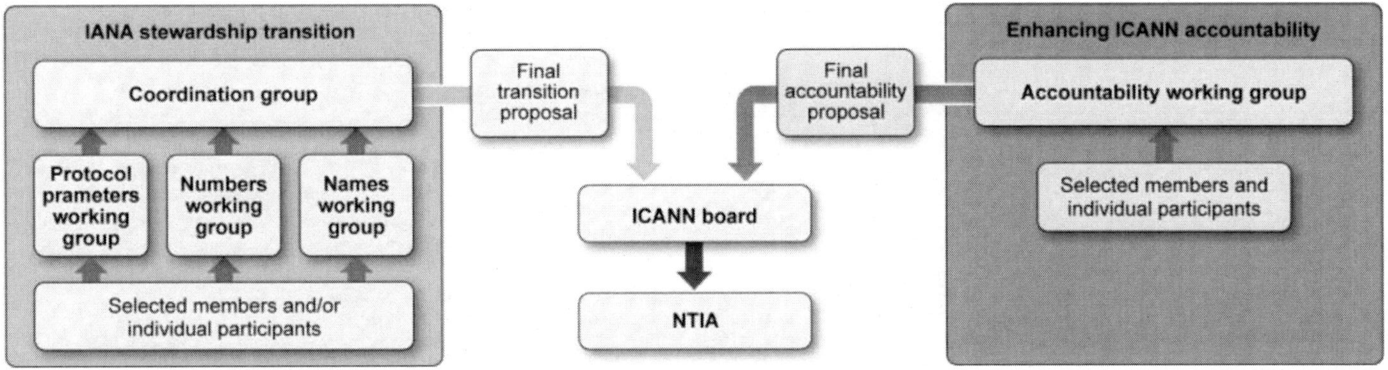

Abbreviations and definitions:

IANA: Internet Assigned Numbers Authority

NTIA: National Telecommunications and Information Administration

ICANN: The Internet Corporation for Assigned Names and Numbers

Accountability working group: Cross Community Working Group on Enhancing ICANN Accountability

Coordination group: The IANA Stewardship Transition Coordination Group

Protocol parameters working group: Planning for the IANA/NTIA Transition

Numbers working group: The Consolidated RIR IANA Stewardship Proposal Team. RIR refers to Regional Internet Registries

Names working group: The Cross Community Working Group to Develop an IANA Stewardship Transition Proposal on Naming Related Functions

Source: GAO analysis of NTIA, ICANN, and working group documents. | GAO-15-642

Figure 7. Summary of Parallel Processes to Develop the Transition Proposal.

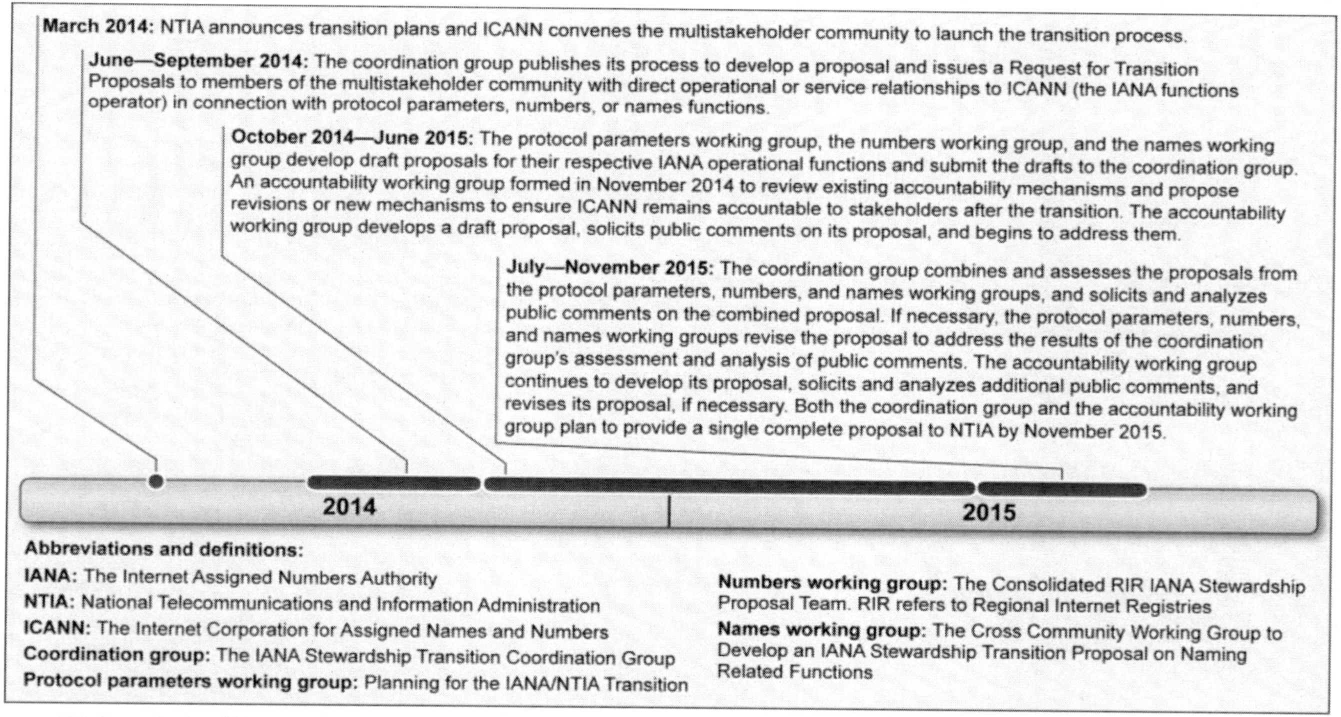

Source: GAO analysis of NTIA, ICANN and community working group documents. | GAO-15-642

Figure 8. Planned Time Frame for the Multistakeholder Community to Deliver a Proposal to Transition from National Telecommunications and Information Administration's Internet Technical Functions Contract, as of July 6, 2015.

The accountability working group published its draft proposal on May 4, 2015, (the recommendations in the draft proposal were not presented as the consensus of the group) for a public comment period that ran until June 12, 2015. After addressing the first round of public comments on the proposal, the accountability working group posted its revised proposal for a second round of public comments from August 3 through September 12, 2015, with the hope of getting the final proposal approved by the group's chartering organizations by the conclusion of the next ICANN meeting in Dublin, Ireland in late October 2015, and submitting the proposal to the ICANN board in November 2015.

Current Time Frame Envisions Proposal Will Be Provided to NTIA by November 2015

Although the coordination group had originally planned for its work to be completed in time to allow the transition to take place before September 30, 2015, when the current contract between NTIA and ICANN expires, NTIA has not viewed this date as a deadline. The NTIA Administrator has indicated on various occasions that it is more important to get the proposal right than to hit a particular target time frame. If necessary, the current contract may be extended for up to 4 years. In recognition of further work to be done and concerns raised by some members of the multistakeholder community regarding whether all necessary tasks can be completed by September 30, 2015, NTIA wrote a letter to the chairs of the coordination group and accountability working group on May 6, 2015. In the letter, NTIA asked for an update on the status of the transition planning, including each community's views regarding how long it will take to finalize the transition plan and implement it after it is approved. Subsequently, at the ICANN meeting in Buenos Aires, the NTIA Administrator estimated that the total time of U.S. government review, including NTIA and potentially congressional review, could be 4-to-5 months.

On July 6, 2015, the chairs of the coordination group and the chairs of the accountability working group responded to NTIA under separate letters. The coordination group's chairs estimated that the coordination group could provide a proposal to NTIA via the ICANN board at the ICANN meeting in Dublin, Ireland, in late October 2015; or in early November 2015. The accountability working group's chairs estimated that the group could provide a proposal to the ICANN board by November 2015, a proposal that they anticipated would be forwarded to NTIA in that same month. Both letters stated that the transition could be completed in the July 2016 time frame. Their estimates included consideration of the 4-to-5-month review period that NTIA had suggested would likely be needed by NTIA and Congress. In their letters, the coordination group chairs stated that they considered their timeline to be optimistic, and the accountability working group chairs suggested that it might be prudent to anticipate the potential need for additional time, such as until September 2016. For more details on the time frame described in these July 6 letters, see Figure 8.

Working Groups' Approaches for Developing Draft Proposals Generally Incorporated Risk Management Principles

While the accountability working group has a broad focus on accountability, ICANN's accountability as it relates to its role for each technical function is also central to the scope of the technical function working groups' proposals, as described in the request for proposals outlined above. As a result, all four working groups discussed ICANN's accountability to their respective community in developing their proposals. In doing so, their efforts all encompassed a consideration of risks related to the proposed transition. In order to consider what, if any, new mechanisms needed to be established to preserve ICANN's accountability without the NTIA contract, the technical function working groups and the accountability working group each held a series of meetings during which they identified and discussed any risks to accountability raised by the transition and, if any risks were identified, considered various new mechanism(s) to address these risks. Their draft proposals include the mechanisms selected through this process.[38]

Neither the coordination working group's request for proposals nor the accountability working group's charter specified that the working groups should use a risk management framework to assess risks. Nevertheless, we found that the working groups' approaches to considering and addressing risks are consistent with general risk-management principles, which help guide a risk management framework. The purpose of a risk management framework is to provide a systematic process to assess threats and take appropriate steps to deal with them. Our risk management framework[39] and others developed by the Committee of Sponsoring Organizations of the Treadway Commission (COSO)[40] and the International Organization for Standardization (ISO)[41] contain similar principles to guide a risk assessment process. We compared the four working groups' approaches to these principles and found that the approaches generally aligned with the principles, as shown in Table 1.

Table 1. Comparison of General Risk Management Principles with Working Groups' Approaches to Considering and Addressing Risks to Transition of National Telecommunications and Information Administration's (NTIA) Role in the Internet Technical Functions

General risk management principles[a]	Working groups' approaches to considering and addressing risks
Define objectives.	The objective of the technical function working groups, as defined in the coordination group's charter, is to propose the arrangements required for the continuance of the Internet technical functions in an accountable and widely accepted manner after the expiration of the contract between the National Telecommunications and Information Administration (NTIA) and the Internet Corporation for Assigned Names and Numbers (ICANN). The accountability working group defined its objective as ensuring that ICANN remains accountable to the needs and expectations of the multistakeholder community after the transition.
Identify and assess risks.	The 3 technical functions working groups identified and assessed risks to ICANN's accountability as operator of the related technical functions in a series of meetings. The accountability working group identified and assessed 37 risks that could threaten ICANN's accountability in a series of meetings and through draft documents that were circulated among the community for review and comment.
Evaluate alternatives, or strategies, for addressing these risks.	For the technical functions working groups, the level of risk to accountability identified determined the extent to which alternatives were evaluated. For example, because the protocol parameters working group determined that NTIA's contract was not key to oversight and accountability, it proposed no new accountability arrangements. In contrast, the numbers and names working groups, which determined that the NTIA contract was an important accountability

Table 1. (Continued)

General risk management principles[a]	Working groups' approaches to considering and addressing risks
	mechanism related to ICANN's operation of the relevant technical functions, each considered alternative structures in working group meetings or draft proposals. In addition, the names working group engaged outside legal counsel to help it evaluate these alternatives. The accountability working group evaluated alternatives for addressing identified risks in draft documents that were discussed by the group. It also engaged outside legal counsel to assist it in evaluating these alternatives.
Select the appropriate alternative(s).	After considering alternative strategies, if applicable, the three technical functions working groups and the accountability working group selected strategies to address identified accountability risks and included them in their draft proposals.
Implement the alternative(s) and monitor the progress made and results achieved.	The accountability working group's draft proposal specifies that certain proposed accountability changes must be in place or committed to before the transition from the NTIA contract can occur. The draft proposal also includes ongoing monitoring and review processes.

Source: GAO analysis of GAO's risk management framework as described in GAO-06-91; the Committee of Sponsoring Organizations of the Treadway Commission, Enterprise Risk Management— Integrated Framework (2004); International Organization for Standardization, ISO 31000 Risk Management—Principles and Guidelines (2009) and ICANN transition working groups' meetings and documents. | GAO-15-642

[a] The principles identified in this table are covered by all three frameworks, although the frameworks are organized using slightly different terms and activities.

The accountability working group, in particular, performed an extensive and documented identification and assessment of risks related to the proposed transition. To do this, the group used what it referred to as a "stress test" methodology, or a series of exercises used to conduct a forward-looking assessment of the potential impact of certain plausible events or scenarios on ICANN's stability and to assess the adequacy of existing and proposed accountability mechanisms available to the multistakeholder community. Specifically, the group identified 37 risks that could threaten ICANN's accountability post-transition and assessed whether existing or proposed mechanisms (accountability measures) in the transition proposal will help to ensure ICANN remains accountable to the multistakeholder community.

The accountability working group gathered and analyzed an inventory of relevant and plausible risks, as identified through public comments. The risks evaluated by the accountability working group's stress test process can be generally categorized as: (1) risks associated with the potential that ICANN could fail to meet operational obligations, such as if ICANN attempts to add a new top-level domain in spite of security and stability concerns expressed by the technical community or other stakeholder groups; (2) risks associated with the potential that ICANN could fail to remain accountable to the multistakeholder community, such as by allowing one stakeholder segment, whether governmental or commercial, to drive its agenda on all other stakeholders or prevent all other stakeholders from advancing their interests; and (3) risks that could threaten ICANN's existence, such as a general financial downturn in the domain name industry, major corruption or fraud at ICANN, or legal or legislative action arising from existing public policy (such as an antitrust suit) which could lead to ICANN's insolvency. The following examples provide a selection of risks that were included in the accountability working group's stress tests, the accountability working group's assessment of the extent to which ICANN would be accountable to the community when facing that risk, and the relevant changes included in the draft proposal and being tested by the accountability working group to support enhanced accountability:

- *ICANN becomes less transparent and accountable in its decision making:* Officials told us that the current affirmation of commitments between NTIA and ICANN is aimed at promoting transparent and accountable budgeting processes, fact-based policy development, and decisions to protect the public interest. Some stakeholders, however, are concerned that absent a contract with NTIA, ICANN may discontinue key commitments and review processes which stakeholders believe help to hold ICANN accountable to the multistakeholder community. For example, ICANN currently has a commitment to undertake community-led reviews relating to accountability and transparency. To address this risk, the accountability working group has proposed changes to ICANN's bylaws that would require ICANN to continue its periodic reviews (at least every 3 years) of: (1) its accountability and transparency; (2) its ability to maintain the security, stability and resiliency of the domain name system; (3) the extent to which new top-level domains promote competition, consumer trust, and consumer choice; and, (4) the effectiveness of its Whois services policy, which, as previously described, requires registrars to document contact information for the registrant of each domain name.

- *ICANN is 'captured' by one or several stakeholder groups:* The multistakeholder model of governance invites participants throughout the world to create shared policies and standards on how the Internet is run. The accountability working group evaluated whether existing or proposed mechanisms would help to manage the risk that ICANN may be 'captured' by one or several groups of stakeholders representing specific sectors. According to some stakeholders we interviewed, this could empower one group of stakeholders to drive an agenda that is not in the interest of global stakeholders—such as governments in the Governmental Advisory Committee seeking to influence policies that would restrict free expression on the Internet at a global level, for example.[42] According to the accountability working group, this risk exists under ICANN's current bylaws. That is, for example, the ICANN board must consider and respond to advice from the Governmental Advisory Committee on the formulation and adoption of public policies—especially where there may be an interaction between ICANN's policies and national laws or international agreements—and must try to find a mutually acceptable solution if the board decides to take an action that is not consistent with the Governmental Advisory Committee's advice. If a mutually acceptable solution cannot be found, the ICANN board must state in its final decision the reasons why it did not follow the advice provided by the Governmental Advisory Committee. Although the Governmental Advisory Committee currently seeks consensus among its membership[43] before providing advice to the ICANN board, according to its operating principles, it may decide at any time to revise its operating procedures.[44] The accountability working group administered a stress test which considered the consequences if the Governmental Advisory Committee were to lower the threshold of agreement required to provide advice to the ICANN board from consensus decisions to a simple majority vote. This would make it easier for one segment of the Governmental Advisory Committee to pass policy recommendations and influence ICANN policies. The accountability working group has proposed changing ICANN's bylaws to make it clear that only consensus advice from the Governmental Advisory Committee would trigger a bylaw-required consultation. According to an NTIA senior policy advisor, NTIA supports this clarification to the bylaws and considers the revision both appropriate and necessary to meet the goal that the transition not yield a government-led or intergovernmental replacement for NTIA's current stewardship role.

- *ICANN relocates to another legal jurisdiction:* The accountability working group views the question of jurisdiction as relevant because it holds ICANN accountable to comply with relevant laws under which ICANN is incorporated. For example, California's Attorney General currently has jurisdiction over California nonprofit entities acting outside the scope of their articles of incorporation.[45] ICANN's current bylaws require ICANN's principal office for conducting business to reside in the State of California. However, the accountability working group determined that, without the NTIA IANA functions contract, existing measures would be inadequate to prevent ICANN's board from amending this bylaw provision and moving, potentially outside the United States. According to the accountability working group, such a change could reduce the ability of third parties—such as Internet users or people with registered websites—to seek legal redress for ICANN's failure to enforce contracts or other actions. The accountability working group determined that one of its proposed measures would help to manage this risk by empowering the community to veto a proposed change to the bylaws.

After taking an inventory of existing accountability mechanisms at ICANN, soliciting input from the community regarding ICANN's responsiveness to the community, and analyzing the results of its stress tests, the accountability working group in its draft proposal preliminarily recommended several changes to bolster the accountability mechanisms in place at ICANN. For example, in its draft proposal, the working group proposed revisions to the bylaws to clarify ICANN's mission, protect the public interest as ICANN carries out its mission, and empower the multistakeholder community in key areas, for example, by establishing a set of fundamental bylaws that could only be amended with prior approval from the community. Other proposed revisions include (1) a reform of existing independent review processes to review ICANN performance and provide redress, if necessary; and (2) enhanced community powers, including the ability of the community to reject ICANN board decisions related to ICANN's strategic plan and budget, approve or veto changes to the ICANN bylaws, and remove individual members or recall the entire ICANN board. The accountability working group stated after a face-to-face meeting at ICANN's 53rd meeting in Buenos Aires in June 2015 that in the comments received on its draft proposal, it had received broad support for the overall accountability architecture proposed. However, the accountability working group recognized that questions remained about a proposed model for community empowerment, and stated that it planned to continue to work to revise the proposal in this area.

Accountability Working Group's Consideration of Risks Generally Covered Risks Identified by Stakeholders We Interviewed

Most nonfederal stakeholders we interviewed were generally supportive of the transition. The risks identified by most stakeholders were consistent with those already identified and assessed by the accountability working group or other working groups. Some stakeholders we interviewed stated that generally, technical risks related to the proposed transition were low, and officials at federal agencies we spoke with at an unclassified level,[46] including several agencies with a national security mission, generally supported the transition and did not identify unmanageable national security risks related to the transition.[47]

Officials from the National Institute of Standards and Technology explained that the specific and limited nature of the technical functions and the distributed and voluntary nature of the Internet, together, help to reduce technical risks. That is, they said that network operators and other customers of the technical functions monitor the performance of various systems supporting the Internet and would quickly identify and resolve problems associated with a malfunction at the top-level domain before an Internet user would notice the problem. They also explained that the Internet was designed to include multiple independent root server operators (13) and hundreds of replicated servers distributed throughout the world to help resolve Internet names to the IP addresses necessary for two devices to communicate. A malfunction of one root server may not have a broad impact because any of the other root servers can perform the same task. Lastly, individual computers store information from recent queries of the domain name system in a local cache file, including records of where to access recently-used top-level domains, which means that the Internet user's computer does not always need access to root servers when resolving an Internet name to an IP address in order, for example, to find a particular website. The protocol parameters, numbers, and names working groups included existing or new mechanisms in their draft proposals that would allow the multistakeholder community to appoint a new IANA functions operator if ICANN does not meet expected performance levels. The groups believe that the ability to separate the IANA functions from ICANN will provide sufficient protections to hold ICANN accountable regarding the IANA technical operations, as they believe it effectively replaces the perceived backstop role of NTIA's contract with ICANN.

Officials at one agency expressed concern that without NTIA's contract, ICANN might be less likely to enforce its contracts with registrars, and that this could reduce Internet reliability and transparency and diminish law enforcement's ability to tackle cybercrime. In particular, officials at this agency stated that the requirement that registrars record accurate contact information of each domain name holder is important to help law enforcement officials investigate and prosecute a range of crimes facilitated by the Internet, including for example, identity theft, credit card and bank fraud, child exploitation crimes, computer intrusions and damage (such as hacking and malware), and intellectual property misuse, among others. Registrar agreements with ICANN establish contractual obligations related to Whois, a system used to identify who is responsible for a website or an IP address. In 2013, ICANN revised its contract with Internet registrars to require that all new registered domain names comply with additional requirements of ICANN policies related to the Whois service, which matches websites to their owner or operator, in an effort to improve the accuracy and overall effectiveness of the Whois system.[48] In order to address this risk, the accountability working group has proposed changes to ICANN's bylaws, as discussed above, which would require periodic reviews to assess the effectiveness of ICANN's Whois services policy. Such a review would include an evaluation of the effectiveness of its implementation, and the extent to which its implementation meets the legitimate needs of law enforcement and promotes consumer trust.

Risks identified by most nonfederal stakeholders we interviewed were also generally consistent with those identified and assessed by the accountability working group. For example, some stakeholders with whom we spoke were concerned that a government or other entity may 'capture' ICANN to drive a political agenda or make decisions that are not in the best interests of the multistakeholder community. The proposed accountability measures to address this risk include empowering the multistakeholder community to veto ICANN budgets and strategic plans or to remove board members or directors in certain instances. Two stakeholders, however, said that this risk is low because of the voluntary nature of the system; stating that if ICANN moved away from core principles such as maintaining a secure and stable Internet, it would be possible for the Internet community to move the technical functions to a different operator.

Additionally, three stakeholders told us that there was a risk that without NTIA having the backstop of the contract, the multistakeholder community itself potentially could be captured by those with particular interests such as particular commercial interests. One stakeholder we spoke with stated that it will be important to consider how to ensure that the multistakeholder community is broad enough so that voices within the community can protect the public interest if and when it may be in conflict with certain commercial interests. According to a stakeholder involved with the accountability working group, the group has considered this risk and to address it has proposed establishing an independent panel. In the accountability working group's draft proposal, any group, person, or entity materially affected by an ICANN action or inaction in violation of ICANN's mission or bylaws would have standing to appeal to this independent panel, and the panel's decisions would be binding on the ICANN board. Officials from NTIA have also said that they intend to remain an active stakeholder, after the transition, though the Governmental Advisory Committee or through other means within the multistakeholder model— for example, by remaining engaged on policy issues related to new generic top-level domains or the Whois service.

Some Stakeholders Identified Risks if the Transition Does Not Occur

Some stakeholders we interviewed were concerned about risks if the transition does not occur. These stakeholders believed that if the transition does not happen this may weaken the credibility of the multistakeholder model of Internet governance and could lead to more pressure around the world for governmental or intergovernmental control over the Internet. Some stakeholders stated that greater governmental control over the Internet could potentially stall innovation, result in slower Internet policymaking, and could fragment the Internet, limiting the openness and interoperability we have today. Officials from the State Department and NTIA have said that while this concern has been relieved somewhat with NTIA's announcement of the proposed transition, international pressure may rise again if the transition does not proceed.

According to officials from NTIA and the U.S. Department of State, pressure from those in support of greater intergovernmental control over these Internet functions subsided after NTIA announced the proposed transition. For example, the April 2014 Global Multistakeholder Meeting on the Future of Internet Governance, also known as NETmundial, convened thousands of stakeholders in São Paulo, Brazil, including government officials and representatives of academic, technical, private sector, and civil society organizations to discuss Internet governance principles. Conference participants recognized the Internet as a global resource that should be managed in the public interest and identified a set of principles that emphasized support for an open multistakeholder model of Internet governance, decision making, and policy formulation, among other principles.

NTIA Has Not Determined How It Will Evaluate the Transition Proposal, but Using a Framework Could Help

NTIA Has Not Determined How It Will Evaluate the Transition Proposal against Its Goals

In its transition announcement, NTIA set out several core goals for a successful transition proposal and subsequently told the multistakeholder community that it expects to receive a single proposal that covers the operation of the technical functions as well as community-identified ways to improve ICANN's accountability. NTIA has also said that all work items identified in the final proposal must be implemented before the contract can end. NTIA officials told us they have not identified a framework to guide their assessment of the final proposal against their core goals. According to NTIA officials, they are waiting to receive the final transition proposal before determining how to evaluate it. NTIA officials told us the contents of the final proposal and the quality of the multistakeholder community's effort to produce it, such as the extent of the stress testing conducted and the feedback from a community-led public comment period, will influence how NTIA evaluates the proposal. In addition, they noted that NTIA supports the bottom-up multistakeholder process for developing the proposal and wants to avoid being overly prescriptive in describing the proposal's requirements. NTIA officials have stated that the proposal and the process used to develop it should be driven by the multistakeholder community. NTIA officials told us they have observed the transition-planning process and participated in some of the working groups' meetings, but officials said they have been careful not to provide specific feedback that could dramatically affect the proposal. At certain points, NTIA officials have commented on the overall direction of the transition process, such as by encouraging stakeholders to coordinate the proposals and offering questions about the complexity of an early proposal draft. In one instance, NTIA officials directly engaged with a working group to provide feedback about a specific proposal element.[49]

NTIA will evaluate the transition proposal on behalf of the U.S. government and plans to involve other agencies in its evaluation, according to NTIA officials. In deciding whether or not to accept the proposal and let the technical functions contract with ICANN expire, NTIA plans to consult with an interagency working group that helped define the core goals for the proposal.[50] NTIA's core goals reflect a consensus view of the U.S. government agencies that participated in the interagency group discussion, according to NTIA officials. NTIA told us that several agencies participate in this group, including, among others, the National Institute of Standards and Technology, the Patent and Trademark Office, the Federal Trade Commission, General Services Administration, the Federal Bureau of Investigation; several components of the Departments of State, Defense, Homeland Security, Justice, and the Treasury; and White House offices, including the National Security Council, Office of Management and Budget, and Office of Science and Technology Policy.[51]

Although NTIA officials stated they have not yet determined how they will evaluate the final transition proposal against NTIA's stated goals, they told us the NTIA Administrator has described examples of what was intended by these goals, which are summarized in Table 2.

Table 2. National Telecommunications and Information Administration (NTIA) Examples Describing Core Goals for the Final Transition Proposal of Internet Technical Functions

NTIA's core goal	Example(s) provided by NTIA
Support and enhance the multistakeholder model	• Open, transparent, bottom-up process to develop proposal • Assurance that any changes to how the Internet technical functions are performed (e.g., changes to the lists of protocol parameters, Internet Protocol (IP) addresses, and top-level domains) are consistent with documented procedures developed through the multistakeholder model
Maintain the security, stability, and resiliency of the Internet's domain name system	• Decentralized, distributed authority structure of the system needs to be preserved so as to avoid single points of failure, manipulation, or capture • Integrity, transparency, and accountability of IP addresses, protocol parameters, and domain names must be preserved • Technical function services need to be resistant to attacks, be able to fully recover from degradation, and be operated in a stable legal environment
Meet the needs and expectations of the global customers and partners	• Clear mechanisms for developing and adhering to customer service levels, including timeliness and reliability • Processes for transparency, accountability, and auditability should be clear • Continued separation of the operation of technical functions from Internet policy development
Maintain the openness of the Internet	• Continued environment in which operation of the technical functions does not interfere with free expression or free flow of information • Maintain global interoperability of the Internet
Not replace NTIA's role with government-led or inter-governmental organization solution	• Support multistakeholder model of Internet governance

Source: GAO summary of NTIA public statements. | GAO-15-642

NTIA has continued to engage with the multistakeholder community as the community works to finalize the components of the transition proposal, asking questions about the potential implications and indicating that the public record must demonstrate how the proposal meets NTIA's core goals. For example, before ICANN's June 2015 meeting in Buenos Aires, NTIA asked the multistakeholder community to consider several questions regarding the potential implications of certain elements contained in the working groups' draft proposals, such as new structures, committees, and a membership model for community empowerment. NTIA also asked about how the working groups planned to address the accountability of ICANN's independent review panel, management, and staff. In addition, during the ICANN public meeting in June 2015, the NTIA Administrator emphasized the importance of a community-validated proposal—such that the public record clearly demonstrates how the proposal satisfies NTIA's core goals and provides the basis for ultimately accepting it. The NTIA Administrator said the public record must reflect the community's understanding of the implications of its proposal, including the consequences of structural changes, and must indicate that the community has considered alternatives and provided evidence for selecting the option in the final proposal.

Most of the nonfederal stakeholders we interviewed generally thought NTIA's core goals for the proposal were appropriate, though some said they were broadly-stated.[52] One stakeholder thought the lack of detail about the core goals was beneficial because it gave the multistakeholder community enough latitude to develop a proposal. Most stakeholders thought that accountability was an important part of the transition, and some stakeholders told us that NTIA's core goals did not explicitly emphasize accountability or did not fully address risks related to external accountability. Some other stakeholders thought that accountability was implied in NTIA's goals. NTIA has stated that it considers accountability improvements to be a key part of the transition and has expressed confidence in the multistakeholder community's work to achieve ICANN's enhanced accountability to the multistakeholder community.

Evaluation Frameworks Could Provide Tools for NTIA's Evaluation of a Final Transition Proposal

Certain existing frameworks have been developed to help organizations meet their goals or requirements and could provide tools for NTIA's evaluation of a final transition proposal. NTIA officials told us they are waiting to receive the final proposal before determining how to evaluate it and have not identified a framework to guide their assessment of the final proposal against their core goals, as described above. While the working groups developing the proposals have coordinated their efforts, NTIA expects to receive a final proposal containing two distinct parts—one for operation of the technical functions and another for accountability.

The final proposal may contain several significant changes to the operation of the technical functions and ICANN's accountability structures, as described below.[53] These changes are likely to create a new organizational environment for the operation of the technical functions. When evaluating the final proposal against its core goals, NTIA will most likely need to assess proposed new structures and processes.[54] As of August 3, 2015, some of the changes proposed by the working groups include:

- **New structures** — The names working group proposed that a separate legal entity be formed as an affiliate of ICANN to serve as the operator for the technical functions.[55] In addition, both the names and numbers working groups proposed a new committee to conduct reviews of the technical functions operator to help ensure performance of the agreed-upon levels of service.
- **New contractual obligations** — The numbers and names working groups have each proposed new contracts to ensure that the technical functions operator would continue to be held accountable to the multistakeholder community in these two technical areas.[56] The two working groups have also each proposed processes by which those contracts could be canceled and the technical functions removed from the technical functions operator in the case of unsatisfactory performance.
- **New governance model** — The accountability working group proposed a formal membership model to help ensure the board's accountability to the multistakeholder community. In this model, referred to as the "sole member model," ICANN's existing supporting organizations and advisory committees would jointly participate to exercise their rights as the single, legal member of ICANN. In meetings and a prior proposal draft, the accountability working group explored numerous other potential structures for exercising community powers to ensure accountability. For example, one alternative considered was a membership model in which ICANN's existing supporting organizations and advisory committees would each form unincorporated associations, and through these associations would exercise rights gained as "members" of ICANN. A "designator" model, in which ICANN's supporting organizations and

advisory committees would each "designate" certain board members and have the power to remove such board members, was also considered as a way to potentially give the community comparable authority without adding new legal entities.

- **Changes to ICANN's bylaws** — The accountability working group proposed several bylaw changes, such as revisions to clarify ICANN's mission, protect the public interest as ICANN carries out its mission, and reform of ICANN's independent review processes. The proposed changes also aim to empower the multistakeholder community, such as by establishing a fundamental set of bylaws that could only be revised based on prior approval of the multistakeholder community. Further, the proposal would change the bylaws to require the reviews currently contained in the affirmation of commitments.

NTIA has stated that it intends to evaluate the final transition proposal against its core goals. NTIA has also acknowledged that the multistakeholder community via ICANN is planning to provide the final proposal in two distinct parts—one for the operation of the technical functions and one for accountability. NTIA's evaluation will therefore involve examining the proposed changes in both parts in order to determine the extent to which its core goals for the transition have been satisfied.

Certain frameworks have been developed as leading practices to help organizations obtain reasonable assurance that their goals and objectives will be met or that they will meet requirements.[57] We have noted that, in general, strengthened governance and accountability standards came about as a result of governance and accountability breakdowns in the nonprofit, federal government, and public company sectors, most notably in the public-company financial scandals that led to the enactment of the Sarbanes-Oxley Act of 2002.[58] In recent years, we have considered certain frameworks in relationship to accountability breakdowns or challenges at a variety of organizations, including the Legal Services Corporation, Smithsonian Institution, the United Nation's World Food Program, and, recently, in the First Responder Network Authority (FirstNet), an independent authority created within NTIA to establish a nationwide public-safety broadband network.[59] These types of frameworks could help NTIA evaluate whether the transition proposal meets its core goals, and could also be helpful in considering accountability mechanisms that are included in the proposal.

We identified two frameworks that NTIA could consider in its evaluation of the final proposal:

- The Committee of Sponsoring Organizations of the Treadway Commission *Internal Control—Integrated Framework* (COSO framework) [60] and the
- International Organization for Standardization's quality management principles (ISO quality management principles).[61]

The COSO framework provides a tool to guide stakeholders in systematically assessing whether an organization has the necessary components in place to achieve its goals as the organization adapts to shifting environments, evolving demands, and new priorities. The ISO quality management principles are intended to guide organizations toward meeting customer requirements and improving their performance. Both frameworks are intentionally flexible so that they can be adapted to an entity's particular structure or purpose. In particular, the COSO framework states that stakeholders should use their judgment in applying the framework and that evaluators should tailor points of focus to fit each entity's facts and circumstances.

Applying a framework for evaluation in considering the final transition proposal could offer certain benefits.[62] First, using a framework could bring a leading practices perspective to a proposal developed through the bottom-up multistakeholder process, helping to broaden confidence in the final proposal. NTIA has endorsed the multistakeholder model and its process of developing and testing the proposal through a bottom-up, community-driven, and iterative process, so applying a framework could demonstrate whether the proposal can withstand examination through a different lens of independently developed leading practices. Doing so could help provide assurance to NTIA and all interested stakeholders that the final proposal will meet NTIA's core goals. In addition, a framework that has been publicly recognized as a useful practice could provide a transparent benchmark. Applying a framework for evaluation may also help point to any gaps that the multistakeholder community could work to address before a decision to let the technical functions contract expire. While there is no external requirement governing how NTIA should approach this task, NTIA's lack of this type of framework to evaluate the proposal could make it difficult for NTIA to fully consider the extent to which the proposal is likely to achieve its goals. Without a framework as a tool to systematically review the proposal and its various new structures and processes, it is unclear how NTIA will determine the extent to which its core goals have been addressed. As a result, NTIA may not be assured that its goals for the transition have been fully addressed and embedded over the long term.

NTIA officials agreed that such frameworks could potentially provide a tool with which to evaluate the proposal. They also said these types of frameworks may be useful to the multistakeholder community as the working groups develop and test their proposals. However, NTIA officials stated that their knowledge of the frameworks was limited and that they had not yet determined what type of structured approach would best help NTIA and the interagency working group evaluate the proposal. They also stated that it was not clear to them whether a framework designed to consider an organization as a whole was an appropriate tool to use to consider the transition proposal, which would be focused on issues related to the transition of the technical functions and ICANN's accountability to the multistakeholder community but would likely not cover all of ICANN's activities. In this regard, we believe that the intentional flexibility built into these frameworks for evaluation would permit NTIA to select elements of the frameworks that are applicable to this circumstance. For example, when evaluating the final transition proposal, NTIA could consider applying relevant elements of the COSO framework and ISO quality management principles in some of the ways described below.

Table 3. Key Components of the Framework Developed by the Committee of Sponsoring Organizations of the Treadway Commission

Component	Description
Organizational environment	The processes and structures that help set the tone for the organization toward accountability, such as how the board of directors carries out its responsibilities and how the organization's structure helps it achieve its goals.
Risk assessment	The identification and analysis of relevant risks that may affect the organization's ability to achieve its objectives, and to manage these risks appropriately.
Accountability activities	The actions (e.g., policies or procedures) an organization puts into place to help achieve its objectives. These activities are particularly aligned with risk assessment and might include a separation of different types of duties.
Information and communication	The concept that relevant information must be identified, obtained, and communicated in a form and time frame in order that people can carry out their responsibilities in achieving the organization's objectives.
Monitoring	A process to assess organizational procedures to ensure their effectiveness. This step is accomplished through ongoing monitoring activities or separate reviews, or a combination of the two.

Source: GAO analysis of the Committee of Sponsoring Organizations of the Treadway Commission's Internal Control—Integrated Framework. | GAO-15-642

by the private sector. At the heart of this vision is a global multistakeholder model of Internet governance. NTIA views the proposed transition of these technical functions as an important sign of the U.S. government following through on its endorsement of the multistakeholder model of Internet governance. Some stakeholders we spoke with echoed this idea, stating that a risk of the transition not moving forward would be renewed international pressure for more government involvement in broader aspects of Internet governance—a change that could potentially lead to a slower decision-making process that could interfere with innovation or a decrease in the Internet's openness and global interoperability.

The four working groups established to develop a transition proposal have worked to identify and assess risks and evaluate alternatives or strategies for addressing these risks. In particular, the accountability working group was created to focus on ensuring that ICANN remains accountable in the absence of its historical contractual relationship with the U.S. government. Through these working groups, the multistakeholder community has proposed or is considering a number of mechanisms to manage identified risks while enhancing ICANN's accountability to the multistakeholder community in the absence of the contract with NTIA. NTIA, with input from an interagency working group, will evaluate the proposal on behalf of the U.S. government. According to NTIA officials, NTIA will evaluate the proposal against its core goals but has not yet determined how to evaluate it or identified a framework to guide its assessment.

Given the extent of changes being considered in the developing transition proposal—changes that are likely to create a new organizational environment for the operation of the technical functions—applying a framework for evaluation could provide valuable tools with which to consider the proposal. As a result of governance and accountability breakdowns in the nonprofit, federal government, and public company sectors, strengthened governance and accountability standards have come about in recent years—and frameworks have been developed as leading practices to help organizations obtain reasonable assurance that their goals and objectives will be met, among other things. Applying such a framework to evaluate the transition proposal could serve as a transparent benchmark and help NTIA determine the strength of the proposal, identify any important weaknesses, and consider the extent to which the final proposal will achieve the core goals for the transition. An evaluation that makes use of a framework may help assure all stakeholders and Congress that NTIA has fully analyzed how the final proposal would manage the potential risks that stakeholders have identified related to the Internet functions before letting NTIA's contract with ICANN expire and completing the transition of these Internet functions that was envisioned decades ago.

RECOMMENDATION FOR EXECUTIVE ACTION

To ensure that NTIA's evaluation of the Internet multistakeholder community's transition proposal fully considers whether the proposal provides reasonable assurance that NTIA's core goals for the transition will be met, we recommend that the NTIA Administrator review relevant frameworks for evaluation, such as the COSO framework and the ISO quality management principles, and use the relevant portions of the frameworks to help evaluate and document whether and how the transition proposal meets NTIA's core goals.

AGENCY COMMENTS

We provided a draft of this report to the Departments of Commerce, Defense, Homeland Security, Justice, and State, and to the General Services Administration for their review and comment.

The Department of Commerce provided written comments on our draft report in a letter dated August 10, 2015. These comments are summarized below. The Department of Commerce concurred with our recommendation and stated that as part of its evaluation, NTIA will use the relevant frameworks we suggested to guide its assessment of the final proposal against core goals. The Department of Commerce also provided technical comments, which we incorporated as appropriate.

The Department of Justice's Federal Bureau of Investigation provided technical comments, which we incorporated as appropriate. The Departments of Defense, Homeland Security, and State and the General Services Administration did not provide comments on the draft report.

Mark L. Goldstein
Director
Physical Infrastructure Issues

APPENDIX I: SCOPE AND METHODOLOGY

To provide background information on the Internet Assigned Numbers Authority (IANA) technical functions covered by the contract between the Department of Commerce's National Telecommunications and Information Administration (NTIA) and the Internet Corporation for Assigned Names and Numbers (ICANN), we reviewed documents related to these technical functions and interviewed technical experts from ICANN, including ICANN's chief technology officer, the Internet Society, the Internet Engineering Task Force, and the National Institute of Standards and Technology. We also attended a presentation given by ICANN's staff for these technical functions that described their work.

To describe the process being used to develop a transition proposal and identify how the process is considering risks associated with the transition as identified by stakeholders, we identified stakeholders through a process described below. We followed transition efforts by ICANN and the multistakeholder community by observing multiple sessions related to the transition at ICANN's 52nd meeting in Singapore in February 2015, and listening to (live or via recording, or via reviewing transcripts or meeting notes) selected meetings held by the accountability working group from December 2014 through June 2015; by the coordination working group between December 2015 and June 2015; by the numbers working group from December 2014 through May 2015; and by the names working group from December 2014 through June 2015. We also reviewed some information from a listserv established by the working group on accountability, in order to understand issues raised and the process used to generate consensus among working group members.

We reviewed relevant documents and draft proposals from each multistakeholder working group (the coordination group, the protocol parameter, numbers, and names working groups, and the accountability working group), including documentation of the stress tests conducted by the working group on accountability, among other things. We reviewed prior GAO work related to ICANN.[66]

We also reviewed relevant documents, including the contract between NTIA and ICANN and ICANN's proposal incorporated by reference into the contract, and NTIA documents related to these Internet technical functions and the proposed transition. We reviewed ICANN documents, including, among others, ICANN's bylaws, ICANN's articles of incorporation, ICANN's budgets from fiscal year 2010 to fiscal year 2015, reports by ICANN-affiliated review committees on ICANN's structure and accountability, and the affirmation of commitments between the Department of Commerce and ICANN.

To identify stakeholders, we selected a nongeneralizable sample of stakeholders that were knowledgeable about ICANN and that had differing positions and interests in the working of the Internet technical functions and the proposed transition to help ensure our analysis and conclusions would cover a variety of viewpoints. Selected stakeholders included the following:

- Federal agencies: We interviewed and/or received written responses to questions from NTIA and 10 other federal entities, the majority of which were involved in an NTIA-convened interagency working group. This group included stakeholders from the Department of Defense's Chief Information Officer, Defense Information Systems Agency, and an additional security-related agency; the Department of Homeland Security's Science and Technology Directorate and National Protection and Programs Directorate; the Department of Justice's Criminal Division and Federal Bureau of Investigation; the State Department; the General Services Administration; and the Federal Communications Commission.
- ICANN: We interviewed ICANN officials, including members of ICANN's management, the ICANN board chair, and one ICANN board member.
- ICANN community: We conducted semi-structured interviews with stakeholders involved with ICANN's working groups, supporting organizations, and advisory committees. These stakeholders spoke to us from their individual perspectives and did not represent the views of the ICANN organization or group with which they were associated, nor are their views generalizable to all stakeholders from their particular communities. In some cases, stakeholders we spoke with had experience related to multiple parts of the multistakeholder community. These stakeholders included the chairs (and in some cases, members or participants) of the IANA Stewardship Coordination Group (coordination group), Planning for the IANA/NTIA Transition (protocol parameters working group), the Consolidated RIR IANA Stewardship Proposal team[67] (numbers working group), the Cross Community Working Group on Names (names working group), and the Cross Community Working Group on Accountability (accountability working group). Stakeholders

interviewed also included chairs, members or participants of the Number Resource Organization, Generic Names Supporting Organization (including each of its four stakeholder groups—commercial, noncommercial, registries, and registrars), Country-code Names Supporting Organization, At-large Advisory Committee, Security and Stability Advisory Committee, and Governmental Advisory Committee. Stakeholders interviewed also included root server operators.

- Others: We also conducted semi-structured interviews with stakeholders from industry groups and associations representing businesses, telecommunications companies, think tanks, and academic institutions with a focus on Internet governance issues and interviewed Internet freedom organizations, and economists with knowledge about ICANN and a perspective on any economic implications of ICANN's technical functions operations or the proposed transition.

In total, we interviewed officials from 10 federal entities outside of the Department of Commerce, and additional stakeholders representing 31 unique stakeholder perspectives. We use indefinite quantifiers throughout the report—"some", "many", and "most"—to inform the reader of the approximate quantity of nonfederal stakeholders that agreed with the particular statement or idea. To determine when to use each indefinite quantifier, we split the total of the nonfederal stakeholders into approximate thirds, so that "some" would refer to more than one but fewer than or about equal to one-third of the respondents (i.e., 2 to 11 of the nonfederal entities); "many" would refer to more than one-third but fewer than or about equal to two-thirds of the respondents (i.e., 12 to 21 of the nonfederal entities); and, "most" would refer to more than two-thirds of the group but not all respondents (i.e., 22 to 30 of the nonfederal entities). The information from these interviews is not generalizable but provides us with a broad perspective from knowledgeable stakeholders on potential risks related to the transition and the multistakeholder community's approach to develop a transition proposal to address potential risks and meet NTIA's core goals.

To further consider how the process to develop a transition proposal is considering risks related to the transition, we compared the processes being used by the transition working groups to identify risks and propose management strategies for these risks to general principles recommended by risk management frameworks developed by us, the Committee of Sponsoring

Organizations of the Treadway Commission (COSO), and the International Organization for Standardization (ISO).[68] We selected these principles and frameworks based in part on our prior work that used these frameworks. In addition, our risk management framework was designed through a broad range of consultations with prior government reports and experts in the fields of risk management, risk modeling, and terrorism, and through reviewing numerous frameworks from industry, government, and academic sources. It was also field tested on several GAO reviews and reviewed by three academic experts in risk management. The other two sets of principles and frameworks we considered were designed by nongovernmental organizations—one by COSO and one by ISO—based on leading practices, with the goal of improving risk management in a broad range of organizations. To determine how NTIA is planning to evaluate a transition proposal against its core goals for the transition, we reviewed documentation on NTIA's core goals and public statements by NTIA that provided some additional detail on these goals. We also interviewed NTIA officials. To identify what, if any, tools could help NTIA with such an evaluation, we summarized the perspectives of stakeholders we interviewed on NTIA's core goals for the transition. We also reviewed our standards for internal control[69] and other prior work, COSO's *Internal Control-Integrated Framework*,[70] and ISO's ISO 9000—*Quality Management Principles and 31000—Risk Management Principles and Guidelines*[71] to evaluate whether these tools could assist NTIA in evaluating a transition proposal in light of its core goals. We selected these frameworks based in part on our prior work that used frameworks from these organizations. Moreover, the COSO framework was designed to be applied across various types of organizations, including nonprofits, and has been recognized as a leading evaluation framework. In addition, the ISO quality management principles provide a framework that can be used to guide organizations toward improved performance and contain guidance and tools that can be used by any type of organization to help meet customer requirements. Both frameworks were developed based on leading practices. We also reviewed these tools for evaluation with NTIA.

We conducted this performance audit from September 2014 to August 2015 in accordance with generally accepted government auditing standards. Those standards require that we plan and perform the audit to obtain sufficient, appropriate evidence to provide a reasonable basis for our findings and conclusions based on our audit objectives. We believe that the evidence obtained provides a reasonable basis for our findings and conclusions based on our audit objectives.

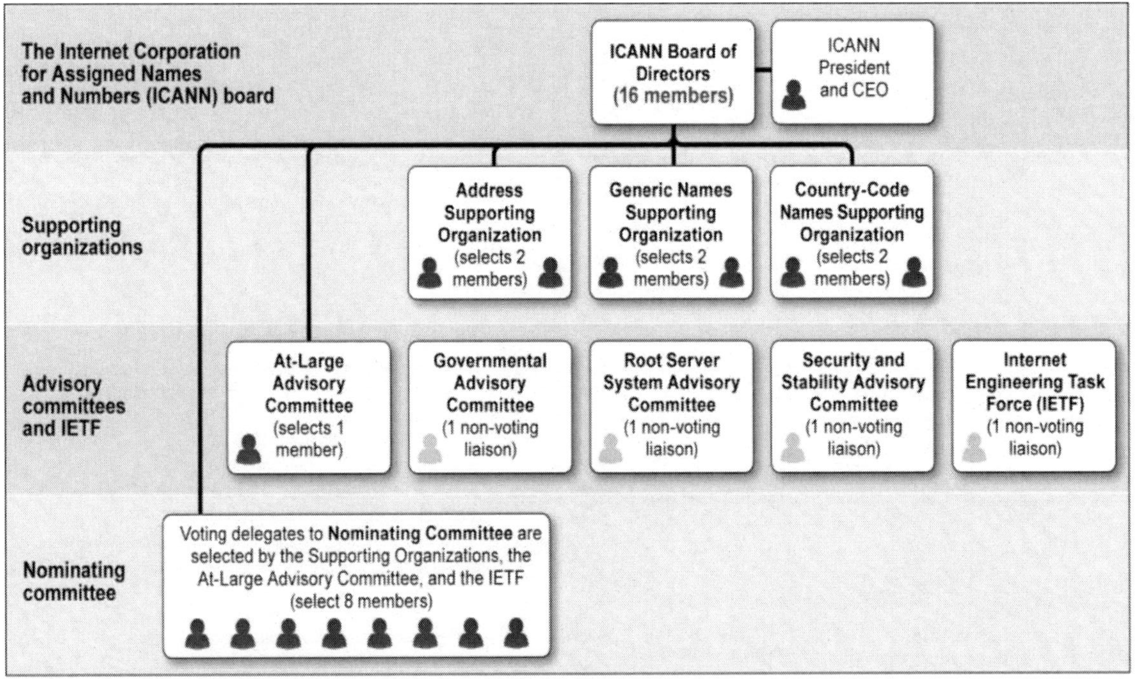

Source: GAO analysis of ICANN bylaws. | GAO-15-642

Figure 9. Board of Directors of the Internet Corporation for Assigned Names and Numbers (ICANN).

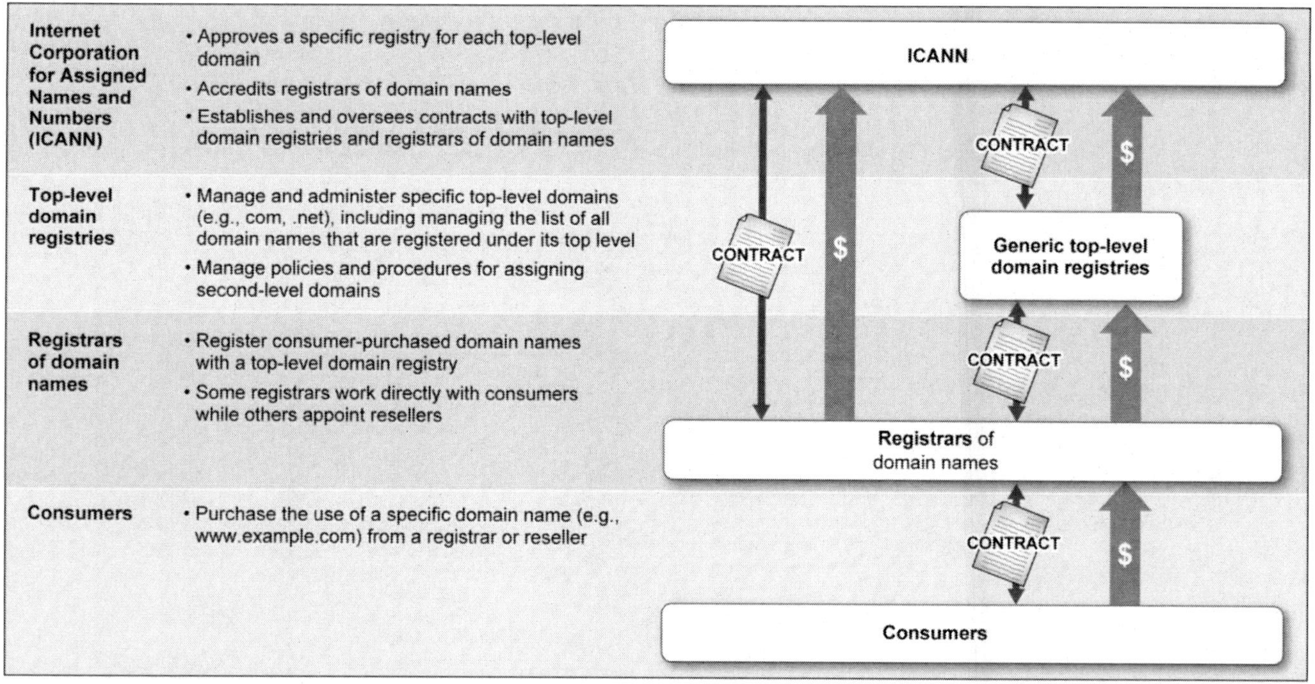

Source: GAO analysis of ICANN information. | GAO-15-642

Figure 10. Business Relationships among the Internet Corporation for Assigned Names and Numbers (ICANN) and Other Parties in the Generic Domain Name Industry.

APPENDIX II: INTERNET CORPORATION FOR ASSIGNED NAMES AND NUMBERS' (ICANN) BOARD, CURRENT ACCOUNTABILITY STRUCTURES, AND CONTRACTS

ICANN's Board and Current Accountability Structures

The board of directors, which oversees the Internet Corporation for Assigned Names and Numbers (ICANN), consists of 16 voting members and four non-voting liaisons. As shown in Figure 9, the voting members of the board are comprised of seven members selected by particular supporting organizations or stakeholder communities, eight members selected by a nominating committee, which is itself made up of individuals from particular stakeholder groups, and the final board member is the president of ICANN. Under the bylaws, no more than five directors can be from the same geographical region and directors are selected to serve three-year, staggered terms.[72]

In addition, ICANN's bylaws specify a number of measures meant to ensure the transparency and accountability of the organization. These include, among other things, maintaining a publicly available website with information on ICANN, including the board's minutes; a notice and comment period for any proposed major policy changes; a reconsideration provision whereby any person or entity materially affected by an action of ICANN may request review or reconsideration of that action by the board; a process for ar independent review of board actions; a periodic review of ICANN structur and operations; and an office of Ombudsman to act as a neutral dispu resolution practitioner.

Contracts and Fees

ICANN has contractual relationships with, and collects fees from, var parties in the generic domain name industry, as shown in Figure 10.

ICANN published an operating-expenses budget of $108 million for year 2015. According to ICANN, its operating revenues primarily come fees paid by top-level domain registries (about 57 percent in fiscal year and registrars (about 40 percent).[73] The contract between NTIA and IC requires that if ICANN charges fees to perform the requirements of the functions contract, those fees be based "on the cost of providing the

service for which the fee is charged." ICANN officials told us that the fees it charges currently are not constrained by this provision in the IANA functions contract because the fees ICANN currently charges are not collected for services that are performed in relation to the IANA functions specified in the contract.

At the end of May 2015, according to ICANN officials, it had 317 staff members in its operations program. In addition to its headquarters in Los Angeles, it has hub offices in Istanbul, Turkey and Singapore, and has engagement offices in Beijing, China; Brussels, Belgium; Geneva, Switzerland; Montevideo, Uruguay; Seoul, Korea; and Washington, D.C.

End Notes

[1] The International Telecommunication Union (ITU) estimates that by the end of 2014, there were about 3 billion Internet users around the world.

[2] These functions are often grouped into three categories: protocol parameters, numbers, and names (the domain name system). We will explain these more fully later in the report.

[3] Some IP addresses have been reserved for technical or other purposes.

[4] The Advanced Research Projects Agency provided funding to establish a research network beginning in the 1960s. Since then, it changed its name to Defense Advanced Research Projects Agency.

[5] The White House, *Memorandum on Electronic Commerce* (July 1, 1997); see also Management of Internet Names and Addresses, 63 Fed. Reg. 31741, 31741 (June 10, 1998) (summarizing the White House Memorandum).

[6] NTIA is the executive branch agency located within the Department of Commerce that is principally responsible for advising the President on telecommunications and information policy issues.

[7] This document is known as the domain name system "*White Paper*." *See* Management of Internet Names and Addresses, 63 Fed. Reg. 31741 (June 10, 1998). Prior to that, NTIA proposed that a private nonprofit entity, operated for the benefit of the Internet as a whole, could coordinate the Internet's technical functions, in a proposal known as the "*Green Paper*." *See* Improvement of Internet Names and Address, 63 Fed. Reg. 8826, 8826 (Feb. 20, 1998).

[8] In 1998, the Department of Commerce's NTIA entered into a memorandum of understanding with ICANN to develop and test the methods for transitioning certain Internet technical functions to the private sector. According to a 1998 policy statement, NTIA intended to remain involved until the new nonprofit was established and stable, and then phase out U.S. government participation within 2 years.

[9] In 2000, NTIA entered into a no-cost-to-the-government contract with ICANN for the performance of these functions. NTIA entered into several subsequent contracts with ICANN, including the current contract, which was awarded through a competitive procurement process in July 2012.

[10] Although the contract expires on September 30, 2015, it contains two option periods that can extend it through September 30, 2019.

[11] Increasingly, devices other than computers are connecting to the Internet. These devices can include cell phones, tablets, vehicles, and home appliances, among many others.

[12] The contract specifies that designated IANA functions staff members will not initiate, advance, or advocate any policy development related to the IANA functions.

[13] The entries in this protocol parameters database are called registries. The registries contain various codes and numbers that describe the possible values for each protocol. According to the IANA department of ICANN, this database contains over 2,800 registries and sub-registries.

[14] The IETF is a large, open international community dedicated to making the Internet work better from a technical standpoint and is the principal body engaged in the development of Internet standards, such as protocols.

[15] Memos in the requests-for-comments (RFC) document series contain technical and organizational notes about the Internet. They cover many aspects of computer networking, including protocols. RFCs for new or revised protocols contain an "IANA consideration" section to specify actions for the technical functions operator in updating the protocol parameters database.

[16] An additional part of the protocol parameters function involves maintaining the top-level domain Address and Routing Parameter Area (ARPA), which is designated for Internet infrastructure purposes, such as reverse mapping of some IP addresses to Internet domain names.

[17] Allocation refers to the distribution of IP address blocks to the regional Internet registries or other organizations for the purpose of further distribution. In addition to IP addresses, ICANN allocates autonomous system numbers to identify networks of computers. These autonomous system numbers are the mechanism to aggregate large groups of computers into single networks, such as that of a specific Internet service provider or organization. In this report, we refer to numbering resources generally as IP addresses.

[18] Regional Internet registries allocate blocks of IP addresses according to policies and procedures developed within their region. As an example, this process may involve allocating blocks of IP addresses to national or local Internet registries, which then assign the address space to Internet service providers. (Assignment refers to the delegation of IP address space to a particular Internet service provider or end user.) An Internet service provider then may assign an IP address to an end user.

[19] In addition, ICANN manages the top-level domain INT, which is used exclusively for cross-national organizations such as the United Nations.

[20] The root zone database is distinct from the authoritative root zone file. According to the IANA functions contract, ICANN shall maintain, update, and make publicly accessible a database with current and verified contact information for all top-level domain registry operators.

[21] ICANN also adds new country-code top-level domains. Eligible country-code top-level domains include those internationally recognized country codes listed in the International Organization for Standardization (ISO) 3166-1. The only exceptions include country codes that have been grandfathered prior to 2000 or those eligible under ICANN Board Resolution 00.74, which includes the code for the European Union.

[22] NTIA does not have an operational role related to the protocol parameters or numbers functions.

[23] Verisign has a separate cooperative agreement with NTIA related to its role as maintainer of the authoritative root zone file.

[24] The White House, *Memorandum on Electronic Commerce* (July 1, 1997).

[25] Two of the supporting organizations are related to the names function—the Generic Names Supporting Organization, which presents policies to the ICANN board related to generic top-level domain names, and the Country-Code Supporting Organization, which presents policies to the ICANN board related to country-code top-level domains. The third is related to the numbers function—the Address Supporting Organization. The supporting organizations have somewhat different roles in part because while names-related policies are developed within the ICANN community, numbers-related policies are developed largely through forums facilitated by the regional Internet registries, which are outside of

ICANN, and then, in the case of global policies, brought to the ICANN community through the Address Supporting Organization. The protocol parameters function does not have a supporting organization. Related policy is developed outside of ICANN through the IETF.

[26] The ICANN bylaws proscribe the particular membership for each advisory committee or supporting organization and the various ways in which members are selected. Each supporting organization and each advisory committee has elected or appointed members and leaders, except the Governmental Advisory Committee. For the Governmental Advisory Committee, membership is open to all national governments, and each government that becomes a member may appoint one representative to the committee.

[27] We testified about transition progress at that time. GAO, *Internet Management: Limited Progress on Privatization Project Makes Outcome Uncertain* GAO-02-805T (Washington, D.C.: June 12, 2002).

[28] These reviews are to cover: (1) ensuring accountability, transparency, and the interests of global Internet users; (2) preserving security, stability, and resiliency of the domain name system; (3) promoting competition, consumer trust, and consumer choice; and (4) ICANN policies regarding the recording of contact information for all registered websites (known as the Whois service).

[29] The first accountability and transparency review, completed in 2010, contained 27 recommendations to enhance activities throughout ICANN, including the governance and performance of the board, the role and effectiveness of the Governmental Advisory Committee, public input and public policy processes, and review mechanisms for board decisions. All recommendations were accepted by the ICANN board and directed to be implemented. The second review, completed in January 2014, determined that ICANN had made good progress in implementing these recommendations but that more remained to be done. This review also made 12 new recommendations related to the same areas. Reviews of security and stability and Whois have also been completed. Community work to support the competition, consumer choice and consumer trust review, to be formally launched this fall, is also under way.

[30] ICANN officials told us that some of these managers are government entities that are not permitted to contract with ICANN, and so this is not a requirement for country-code top-level domain managers.

[31] ICANN holds three public meetings a year in different locations around the world. At these meetings, stakeholders, supporting organizations, and advisory committees come together to discuss policy issues. Interested parties are invited to observe these discussions in-person or via remote participation.

[32] See: ICANN. *Transition of NTIA's Stewardship of the IANA Functions: Process to Develop the Proposal and Next Steps*, accessed May 4, 2015, https://www.icann.org/resources/pages/process-next-steps-2014-06-06-en.

[33] The coordination group, formally called the IANA Stewardship Transition Coordination Group, is comprised of 30 individuals representing 13 communities of stakeholders, including communities with direct operational or service relationships with ICANN (as IANA functions operator) and other stakeholders from governments, Internet users and businesses. A full list of members has been published on ICANN's website: https://www.icann.org/resources/pages/coordination-group-2014-06-17-en.

[34] Officially called the Cross Community Working Group on Enhancing ICANN Accountability, the accountability working group consists of 26 members, including 24 members selected by the group's chartering organizations, an ICANN staff representative, and an ICANN board liaison. The accountability working group's charter was adopted by the Generic Names Supporting Organization, the Country-Code Names Supporting Organization, the Address Supporting Organization, the At-Large Advisory Committee, and the Governmental Advisory Committee.

[35] The three technical function working groups include (1) the protocol parameters working group, officially called the Planning for the IANA/NTIA Transition working group; (2) the

numbers working group, officially called the Consolidated RIR IANA Stewardship Proposal Team (RIR refers to regional Internet registry); and (3) the names working group, officially called the Cross Community Working Group to Develop an IANA Stewardship Transition Proposal on Naming Related Functions.

[36] The protocol parameters working group consists of participants in IETF. The numbers working group's members were selected by the five regional Internet registries. The names working group's members were selected by the group's chartering organizations. The membership includes representatives from the At-Large Advisory Committee, the Country Code Names Supporting Organization, the Governmental Advisory Committee, the Generic Names Supporting Organization, and the Security and Stability Advisory Committee. In addition to members, interested parties may participate in or observe the process of developing the transition proposal.

[37] For coordination group archives, see: https://www.icann.org/resources/pages/icg- archives-2014-07-31-en; for the protocol parameters community archives, see: http://www.ietf.org/mail-archive/web/ianaplan/current/maillist.html; for the numbers community archives, see: https://www.nro.net/nro-and-internet-governance/iana-oversight/consolidated-rir-iana-stewardship-proposal-team-crisp-team; for the names community archives, see: https://community.icann.org/display/gnsocwgdtstwrdshp/Meetings; and, for the accountability working group, see: https://community.icann.org/display/acctcrosscomm/Meetings.

[38] The protocol parameters working group established that under the current arrangement, oversight and accountability for the protocol parameters functions is carried out by the Internet Architecture Board and IETF. It determined that because the current system works well with no operational involvement from NTIA, no new structures or organizations are required.

[39] GAO, *Risk Management: Further Refinements Needed to Assess Risks and Prioritize Protective Measures at Ports and Other Critical Infrastructure,* GAO-06-91 (Washington, D.C.: Dec. 15, 2005). We developed a risk management framework by reviewing risk literature and previous GAO reports and testimonies. We also consulted, among other things, the Government Performance and Results Act of 1993; the *Government Auditing Standards*, 2003 Revision; GAO's *Standards for Internal Control in the Federal Government* (November 1999); the work of the President's Commission on Risk Management; and the enterprise risk-management approach of COSO. In addition, we consulted with experts in the fields of risk management, risk modeling, and terrorism; and reviewed numerous frameworks from industry, government, and academic sources. The framework was field tested on several GAO reviews and reviewed by three academic experts in risk management.

[40] Committee of Sponsoring Organizations of the Treadway Commission, *Enterprise Risk Management—Integrated Framework* (2004). COSO is a voluntary private-sector organization dedicated to improving organizational performance and governance through effective enterprise risk management, among other things. According to COSO, a key objective of this framework—which has become widely accepted—is to help managements of businesses and other entities better deal with risk in achieving an entity's objectives.

[41] International Organization for Standardization, *ISO 31000 Risk Management—Principles and Guidelines* (2009). ISO is intended to be a family of standards relating to risk management codified by the International Organization for Standardization, an independent, nongovernmental organization that develops and publishes voluntary international standards. The purpose of *ISO 31000 Risk Management—Principles and Guidelines* is to provide principles and generic guidelines on risk management. *ISO 31000* seeks to provide a universally recognized paradigm for practitioners and companies employing risk management processes to replace the myriad of existing standards, methodologies, and paradigms that differed between industries, subject matters, and regions.

[42] Some countries currently establish policies to restrict Internet content within their national borders.

[43] Membership of the Governmental Advisory Committee is open to all national governments and to distinct economies as recognized in international fora. Multinational governmental organizations and treaty organizations may also participate as observers, on the invitation of the Governmental Advisory Committee through the Chair. As of August 3, 2015, ICANN's website states that the Governmental Advisory Committee has 150 Members, including a Chair and five Vice Chairs, and 32 Observers. According to the Governmental Advisory Committee's Operating Principles, consensus is understood to mean the practice of adopting decisions by general agreement in the absence of any formal objection.

[44] This policy is in the Committee's operating principles, which can be revised at any time.

[45] ICANN is a nonprofit public benefit corporation in California. ICANN does not have shareholders but is governed by a board of directors, through its bylaws, articles of incorporation, and other relevant laws.

[46] Evaluating any security risks at a classified level was outside of the scope of our review. According to NTIA officials, NTIA has established a system whereby officials in the interagency working group, described later in this report, can bring to NTIA any classified concerns related to the proposed transition of the NTIA contract with ICANN. NTIA officials told us that no classified concerns have been brought to their attention through this system.

[47] Officials at the Federal Communications Commission did not comment on this, as they viewed the topic as outside of the scope of their responsibilities. Officials from one federal agency with a national security mission added that due to the complexity and unprecedented nature of this issue, the agency was not able to assess any future impacts to national security. In a letter to congressional defense committees dated July 8, 2015, the Department of Defense stated that it has been and will remain engaged in the interagency group and that the interagency group, led by NTIA and the National Security Council, has been engaged in monitoring the progress of this transition and the related accountability enhancement initiatives.

[48] We previously reported concerns about the accuracy of contact information See GAO-06-165 *Internet Management: Prevalence of False Contact Information for Registered Domain Names* (Washington, D.C.: Nov. 4, 2005). One agency we spoke with expressed continued concerns about ICANN's contract compliance efforts related to the 2013 Internet registrar contract. While we include this information for contextual purposes, analyzing this issue was outside of the scope of our review.

[49] In a posting on the accountability group's mailing list, an NTIA official provided the U.S. government's position that a particular stress test was both appropriate and necessary. The stress test considered the risk of a proposed bylaw change regarding how the ICANN board is required to consider advice from the Governmental Advisory Committee, in order that a lower voting threshold would be needed to provide advice.

[50] NTIA regularly convenes an interagency working group that focuses on Internet domain name system topics.

[51] While NTIA plans to invite the interagency working group to comment on and help evaluate the final proposal, NTIA officials said they cannot require federal agencies to participate in this evaluation. Agencies participate in this group as they deem appropriate, depending on the particular topics discussed at each meeting.

[52] Regarding stakeholder views of NTIA's core goals, we report only on the perspectives of nonfederal stakeholders because most of the federal agencies we interviewed had participated in developing the core goals as part of NTIA's interagency working group.

[53] The protocol parameters working group proposed no new structures in its transition proposal.

[54] NTIA officials told us they intend to consider the accountability part of the proposal as it affects the operation of the Internet technical functions going forward.

[55] Relevant ICANN staff, resources, processes, and data would be transferred to the new entity.

[56] The numbers working group proposed a new contract between ICANN and the five regional Internet registries, including an option to remove the numbers technical functions from

ICANN and appoint a new numbers function operator if needed. The names working group proposed a contract between ICANN and the working group's proposed new entity for operating the technical functions. The names working group also proposed a process through which the technical functions could be removed from this new entity if reviews by committees made up of participants from the multistakeholder community found its performance unsatisfactory. Not yet determined is whether the other technical functions communities (protocol parameters and numbers) would contract directly with this new entity proposed by the names community or with ICANN, and how that might change the final proposal.

[57] These internal control frameworks provide a systematic way to evaluate the extent to which an organization has developed plans to achieve its goals or meet requirements.

[58] See GAO, *Legal Services Corporation: Governance and Accountability Practices Need to be Modernized and Strengthened*, GAO-07-993 (Washington, D.C.: Aug. 15, 2007).

[59] See GAO-07-933; GAO, *World Food Program: Stronger Controls Needed in High-Risk Areas,* GAO-12-790 (Washington, D.C.: Sept. 13, 2012), *Smithsonian Institution: Board of Regents Has Implemented Many Governance Reforms, but Ensuring Accountability and Oversight Will Require Ongoing Action*, GAO-08-632 (Washington, D.C., May 15, 2008); and *Public-Safety Broadband Network: FirstNet Should Strengthen Internal Controls and Evaluate Lessons Learned*, GAO-15-407 (Washington, D.C.: Apr. 28, 2015).

[60] Committee of Sponsoring Organizations of the Treadway Commission, *Internal Control—Integrated Framework* (2013). COSO issued its original framework: "Internal Control—Integrated Framework" in 1992 to help businesses and other entities assess and enhance their internal control. Since that time, COSO's internal control framework has been recognized by regulatory standards setters and others as a comprehensive framework for evaluating internal control.

[61] International Organization for Standardization, *ISO 9000 Quality Management Principles* (2012). ISO is an independent, nongovernmental organization that develops and publishes voluntary international standards. The *ISO 9000* series addresses various aspects of quality management. In particular, *ISO 9001* can be used by internal and external parties and sets the requirements of a quality management system that meets customer needs. It complements *ISO 9004*, which provides a wider focus on quality management, and addresses the needs and expectations of all interested parties by the systematic and continual improvement of the organization's performance.

[62] Evaluating the extent to which the final transition proposal achieves NTIA's core goals and contains measures to keep ICANN accountable to a broad multistakeholder community is beyond the scope of this report.

[63] See, for example, GAO-12-790 and GAO, *District of Columbia Opportunity Scholarship Program: Actions Needed to Address Weaknesses in Administration and Oversight*, GAO-13-805 (Washington, D.C.: Sept. 30, 2013).

[64] The eight ISO quality management principles are: customer focus, leadership, involvement of people, process approach, system approach to management, continual improvement, factual approach to decision making, and mutually beneficial supplier relationships.

[65] ICANN officials have not yet implemented these principles across the organization.

[66] GAO, *Internet Management: Limited Progress on Privatization Project Makes Outcome Uncertain*, GAO-02-805T (Washington, D.C.: June 12, 2002); and GAO, *Department of Commerce: Relationship with Internet Corporation for Assigned Names and Numbers*, GAO/OGC-00-33R (Washington, D.C.: July 7, 2000).

[67] RIR refers to regional Internet registry.

[68] See GAO, *Risk Management: Further Refinements Needed to Assess Risks and Prioritize Protective Measures at Ports and Other Critical Infrastructure,* GAO-06-91 (Washington, D.C.: Dec. 15 2005); Committee of Sponsoring Organizations of the Treadway Commission, *Enterprise Risk Management—Integrated Framework* (2004); and

International Organization for Standardization, *ISO 31000 Risk Management—Principles and Guidelines* (2009).

[69] GAO, *Standards for Internal Control in the Federal Government*, GAO/AIMD-00-21.3.1 (Washington, D.C.: November 1999). These standards were recently updated. The updated standards will be in effect for federal agencies beginning in fiscal year 2016. GAO, *Standards for Internal Control in the Federal Government*, GAO-14-704G (Washington, DC: September 2014).

[70] Committee of Sponsoring Organizations of the Treadway Commission, *Internal Control—Integrated Framework* (2013).

[71] International Organization for Standardization, *ISO 9000 Quality Management Principles* (2012); and *ISO 31000 Risk Management—Principles and Guidelines* (2009).

[72] For purposes of ensuring board member diversity, ICANN divides the world into five regions: Africa, Asia/Australia/Pacific, Europe, Latin America/Caribbean Islands, and North America.

[73] According to ICANN's Chief Financial Officer, these percentages are as of March 2015, based on 9 months of activity in fiscal year 2015. The rest of ICANN's operating revenues come from contributions from the 5 regional Internet registries, country-code top-level domains, meeting sponsorships, and other sources. In addition to this budget, ICANN projected additional revenues of $54.9 million in fiscal year 2015 from new generic top- level domain application fees.

- The Committee of Sponsoring Organizations of the Treadway Commission *Internal Control—Integrated Framework* (COSO framework) [60] and the
- International Organization for Standardization's quality management principles (ISO quality management principles).[61]

The COSO framework provides a tool to guide stakeholders in systematically assessing whether an organization has the necessary components in place to achieve its goals as the organization adapts to shifting environments, evolving demands, and new priorities. The ISO quality management principles are intended to guide organizations toward meeting customer requirements and improving their performance. Both frameworks are intentionally flexible so that they can be adapted to an entity's particular structure or purpose. In particular, the COSO framework states that stakeholders should use their judgment in applying the framework and that evaluators should tailor points of focus to fit each entity's facts and circumstances.

Applying a framework for evaluation in considering the final transition proposal could offer certain benefits.[62] First, using a framework could bring a leading practices perspective to a proposal developed through the bottom-up multistakeholder process, helping to broaden confidence in the final proposal. NTIA has endorsed the multistakeholder model and its process of developing and testing the proposal through a bottom-up, community-driven, and iterative process, so applying a framework could demonstrate whether the proposal can withstand examination through a different lens of independently developed leading practices. Doing so could help provide assurance to NTIA and all interested stakeholders that the final proposal will meet NTIA's core goals. In addition, a framework that has been publicly recognized as a useful practice could provide a transparent benchmark. Applying a framework for evaluation may also help point to any gaps that the multistakeholder community could work to address before a decision to let the technical functions contract expire. While there is no external requirement governing how NTIA should approach this task, NTIA's lack of this type of framework to evaluate the proposal could make it difficult for NTIA to fully consider the extent to which the proposal is likely to achieve its goals. Without a framework as a tool to systematically review the proposal and its various new structures and processes, it is unclear how NTIA will determine the extent to which its core goals have been addressed. As a result, NTIA may not be assured that its goals for the transition have been fully addressed and embedded over the long term.

NTIA officials agreed that such frameworks could potentially provide a tool with which to evaluate the proposal. They also said these types of frameworks may be useful to the multistakeholder community as the working groups develop and test their proposals. However, NTIA officials stated that their knowledge of the frameworks was limited and that they had not yet determined what type of structured approach would best help NTIA and the interagency working group evaluate the proposal. They also stated that it was not clear to them whether a framework designed to consider an organization as a whole was an appropriate tool to use to consider the transition proposal, which would be focused on issues related to the transition of the technical functions and ICANN's accountability to the multistakeholder community but would likely not cover all of ICANN's activities. In this regard, we believe that the intentional flexibility built into these frameworks for evaluation would permit NTIA to select elements of the frameworks that are applicable to this circumstance. For example, when evaluating the final transition proposal, NTIA could consider applying relevant elements of the COSO framework and ISO quality management principles in some of the ways described below.

Table 3. Key Components of the Framework Developed by the Committee of Sponsoring Organizations of the Treadway Commission

Component	Description
Organizational environment	The processes and structures that help set the tone for the organization toward accountability, such as how the board of directors carries out its responsibilities and how the organization's structure helps it achieve its goals.
Risk assessment	The identification and analysis of relevant risks that may affect the organization's ability to achieve its objectives, and to manage these risks appropriately.
Accountability activities	The actions (e.g., policies or procedures) an organization puts into place to help achieve its objectives. These activities are particularly aligned with risk assessment and might include a separation of different types of duties.
Information and communication	The concept that relevant information must be identified, obtained, and communicated in a form and time frame in order that people can carry out their responsibilities in achieving the organization's objectives.
Monitoring	A process to assess organizational procedures to ensure their effectiveness. This step is accomplished through ongoing monitoring activities or separate reviews, or a combination of the two.

Source: GAO analysis of the Committee of Sponsoring Organizations of the Treadway Commission's Internal Control—Integrated Framework. | GAO-15-642

COSO Framework

The COSO framework was designed to be applied across various types of organizations, including nonprofits, and has been recognized as a leading evaluation framework. In prior work, we have used this framework to determine the extent to which various organizations have policies and procedures in place that provide reasonable assurance that the organization will meet its objectives.[63] In this work, we have applied COSO components and found that weaknesses in these areas limit assurance that the organization will achieve its goals. Table 3 describes the key components of the COSO framework. COSO suggests tailoring its framework to fit the entity's circumstances.

When evaluating the final transition proposal NTIA could apply relevant components of the COSO framework in some of the ways described below.

- **Organizational environment:** NTIA could consider how the proposed changes—such as the potential new entity, committees, and membership structure—would modify the organizational environment for the technical functions going forward. Examining the overall environment created by such proposed structures could help NTIA determine the extent to which its core goals for the transition have been satisfied.
- **Risk assessment:** NTIA could use this component to evaluate the combined efforts of all four working groups related to risk. Working groups have proposed various accountability activities related to their own areas of concern—such as the contractual relationship between ICANN and a new entity proposed by the names working group, an entity that could be severed in the event of unsatisfactory service. Using a framework could help NTIA consider the extent to which the multistakeholder community identified risks to NTIA's core goals and the extent to which proposed mechanisms serve as appropriate accountability activities to manage those risks.
- **Monitoring:** NTIA could use this component to consider the various monitoring requirements proposed and determine the extent to which the proposal incorporates sufficient monitoring requirements to help achieve NTIA's core goals over the longer term. For example, the draft accountability proposal contains changes to ICANN's bylaws that would incorporate the reviews that are currently required by the affirmation of commitments.

ISO Quality Management Principles

The ISO quality management principles provide a framework that can be used to guide organizations toward improved performance. These principles contain guidance and tools that can be used by any type of organization to help meet customer requirements.[64] According to ICANN's board and management, the ISO quality management principles are among the best practices for the management of nonprofit and corporate entities that they have considered in the management of ICANN.[65] These principles include a customer focus and a system approach to management, and may provide another tool that could help NTIA systematically consider the final transition plan against its core goals. For example, NTIA could apply certain ISO quality management principles in the ways described below.

- **Customer focus:** Applying this principle typically leads to ensuring that the organization's objectives are linked to customers' needs and expectations, according to ISO. In addition, a customer focus can help ensure a balanced approach between satisfying customers and other interested parties. One of NTIA's core goals is that the transition proposal meets the needs and expectations of the global customers of the Internet technical functions. NTIA could use the ISO principle of customer focus to ask questions and help determine the extent to which the final transition proposal has satisfied this core goal.
- **System approach to management:** Identifying, understanding, and managing interrelated processes as a system helps an organization achieve its objectives and is intended to provide confidence to interested parties about the approach, according to this ISO principle. The final transition proposal will likely introduce processes for managing the technical functions and ensuring accountability—some of which will apply to one particular community, but all of which must work together smoothly in a post-transition environment. NTIA could use this principle to help examine the extent to which the final transition proposal manages potentially interrelated processes and develops a coherent approach to meeting NTIA's core goals.

CONCLUSIONS

The U.S. government has long envisioned that the operation of the basic Internet technical functions known as the IANA functions would be managed

INDEX

A

B

C

N

O

P

Q

R

S

T

U

V

W

Y